AF260806

CLOTHED WITH BEAUTY

Clothed

with

Beauty

A CATHOLIC
PHILOSOPHY OF DRESS

ANNA KALINOWSKA

Os Justi Press
P.O. Box 21814
Lincoln, NE 68542
www.osjustipress.com

Send inquiries to
info@osjustipress.com

ISBN 978-1-965303-79-5 (paperback)
ISBN 978-1-965303-80-1 (hardcover)

Book Design by Michael Schrauzer
Cover image: Illustration from Boccaccio's
Des cleres et nobles femmes, depicting Pamphile (Παμφίλη),
a woman of the Greek island of Kos, who Pliny the Elder
says was the first to weave silk. Image: https://gallica.
bnf.fr/ark:/12148/btv1b10515437z/f83.item.zoom

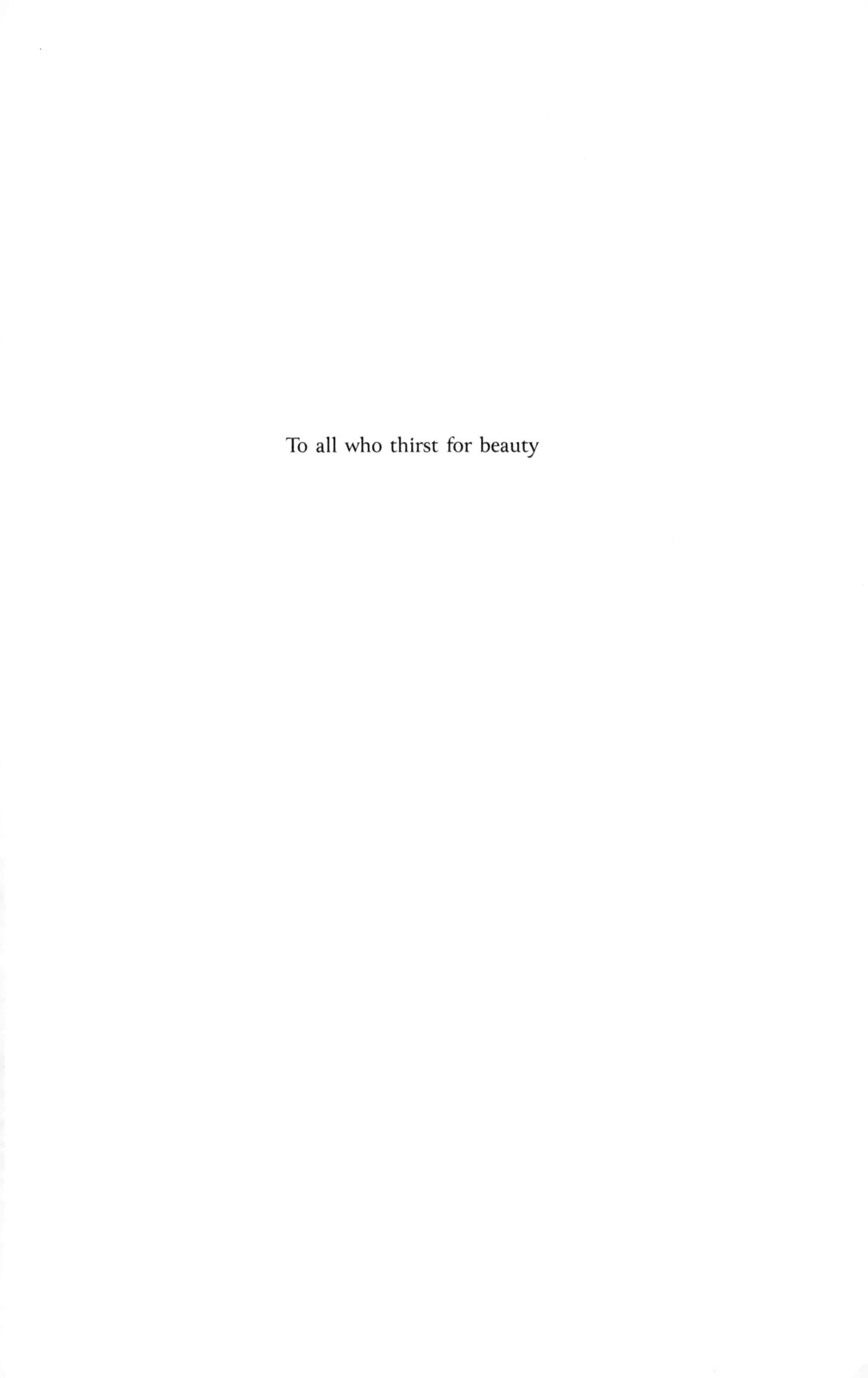

To all who thirst for beauty

CONTENTS

PREFACE

AS A LITTLE GIRL, I USED TO PULL the *F* volume of the family encyclopedia and pore intently over its three or four pages of fashion history. They contained neat rows of illustrated figures modeling clothing from ancient times up to the '80s when the volumes were published. I don't recall, however, giving much attention to anything after the '60s. Those later illustrations were all drab, boxy shapes and blunt lines—too much like the clothing of the '90s and 2000s, which I knew and disliked. Within the splendid array of older costumes, the ones with the long skirts and the big poofs, I never could decide on a favorite. Feeling vaguely wistful, I could only close the volume and return it to its place. Never mind which era was best; any era, it seemed to me, was better than the present day.

It wasn't just queens and princesses I envied either. When my mother supplied me and my sisters with Tom Tierney coloring books, I realized that I loved the clothing of nobility and peasants alike. Coloring away, I'd wonder why even my best clothing was so markedly inferior to that of the poorest Tierney peasants.

At the time, I could only conclude that the older clothes appealed to me simply *because* they were older. One hundred years from now, a girl would look back wistfully on my Cardinals T-shirt and jeans just as I looked back wistfully on the shirtwaists and trumpet skirts of the Edwardians. It was absurd reasoning, but I still believed then that clothing had developed through history on a continuum as smooth and inevitable as those orderly rows lined up in my encyclopedia, starting with togas and running straight to my own day.

Thus, I resigned myself to dressing as well as I could in the standard market fare. Far be it from me to rebel against the inevitable course of history. My entry into the corporate world saw me adopt a corporate chic style—the kind churned out by Ann Taylor Loft, White House Black Market, and the like. I tried to content myself with blunt pencil skirts and boxy blazers, all the while knowing I didn't look any better than those modern figures in my encyclopedia.

Then, in my mid-twenties, I discovered the Traditional Latin Mass. The experience for me, a cradle Catholic who had always attended Holy Mass, was nonetheless a conversion. Scales fell from my eyes, and I found answers to many questions—even, as it turned out, on matters of dress. It struck me that the new liturgy with which I was so familiar had not come to me through the ages on a continuum, but was, rather, the mangled remains of something that had, in recent history, been ripped up by the roots and replanted in a sorry way. If such a cataclysmic rupture could befall the liturgy, the highest of all arts, it seemed to me that no lower art (even everyday dress) would have escaped the aftershocks. To link the Second Vatican Council to the downfall of the art of dress oversimplifies the case, but whether one pins the time of dress's demise to the Council, the Sexual Revolution, the First World War, or the Industrial Revolution, the fact is clear enough: art fell off a cliff in recent history. Hence, the abysmal state of dress. Finally, it came home to me that my discontent with contemporary dress was no silly nostalgia for older ways; it was merely a recognition of bad art.

I discovered that just as there were objective principles that guided true liturgical development, there were objective principles that guided the art of dress. Until the point of rupture, those principles permeated every historical era—all the ones I admired in my encyclopedia—not restricting artists to bland variations of the same modes, but opening to them, like keys in so many locks, the vast and wildly diverse possibilities of beauty.

My study of aesthetics in light of this discovery brought me to fine philosophers like Eric Peterson, Roger Scruton, and Dietrich von Hildebrand, who discuss the fall of great art forms like liturgy, music, and architecture. But I found no Catholic works focused directly on dress that espoused the idea of rupture and the need for restoration while putting forward, in no uncertain terms, artistic principles. Admittedly, several books on dress written by Catholic women have recently been published, but these do not approach the subject in terms of principles or historical analysis. Their focus is on promoting feminine dignity and helping women through insecurities. Lauding normalcy and relevance, they mention neither rupture nor restoration. At most, they speak of the role dressing attractively may play in the New Evangelization, but this notion is always presented as a justification for embracing, rather than rejecting, the modes of the present day. I found these books disappointing.

Thus, making no claim to having developed an original aesthetical philosophy, but having examined dress in the light cast by thinkers greater than myself, I put forward this book as my small contribution to the work of restoration. To restore the art of dress, i.e., to build a culture that practices the art with an eye for the good and the beautiful, and not just the comfortable and convenient, is an endeavor staggering in its scope. After all, dress is an art practiced by every man, woman, and child, prolifically and relentlessly, and, at present, very badly. How does one halt the ever-plunging descent? And if one can succeed in that, how does one begin the upward climb? In the face of such questions, a slender book seems a paltry solution. Nevertheless, the longing for beauty written on every human heart may be a powerful force when awakened. My hope is to enliven in the hearts of readers this innate longing and inspire them to imitate, in each act of dress, their heavenly Creator Who creates nothing that is not beautiful.

This work might never have made it to print at all if I had not received the greatest encouragement and practical assistance from many dear friends and mentors. My very special gratitude goes to my parents, Robert and Barbara Kalinowski, Dr. Peter Kwasniewski, Kenneth Colston, Kristin Kalinowska, Katie Kalinowska, Andrew and Gwyneth Thompson-Briggs, Zachary Thomas, John Fogarty, Lauren Hoijarvi, and Timothy Flanders. Earlier versions of several chapters were published at *OnePeterFive* and are included here with permission.

The title of this book is taken from Psalm 92:1: "The Lord hath reigned, He is clothed with beauty: the Lord is clothed with strength, and hath girded Himself." Since we are made "to the image and likeness of God," it behooves us to be, like Him, clothed in beauty and strength.

St. Louis, Missouri
The Nativity of Our Lady
Year of Jubilee, 2025

I

Predominant Schools of Thought

THERE ARE, AMONG DEVOUT CATHO-lics, generally two ways of thinking about dress. The first way expounds modesty as the highest aim: if only we cover what ought to be covered, then we really need not, and perhaps should not, trouble ourselves much more about dress. The second way, partially in response to the unattractive results often produced by the first, values normalcy above all else: we Catholics can, they say, look normal; we can even enjoy following modern fashions.

But both schools of thought leave out something critical to a proper understanding of dress—namely, that dress is an art.

While the School of Modesty teaches important lessons on safeguarding chastity, its adherents often fall short of artistic success simply because they do not consider artistic principles. A bit like the painting instructor who never moves past the introductory lesson on the dangers of turpentine, students of this school never learn how delightful dress can be and how beautiful its results. They tend to view dress as a moral science, full of litmus tests involving measurements of two fingers' breadth, arm waving, bending over, and fabric pinching. Their idea of success is meeting certain criteria drawn up like a school dress code, which they believe is demanded by a Vatican document, the writing of a particular saint, or the words of a zealous parish priest.

The School of Normalcy has grown up partially as a backlash against the School of Modesty and partially as a misguided attempt to despoil the Egyptians. We can embrace modern trends, adherents of normalcy claim, and turn them to the good. By looking normal, we may attract others.

But it's critical to remember that despoiling the Egyptians is only advisable when the Egyptians possess something worth despoiling. The Israelites took Pharoah's gold, a precious substance, easily converted from idols to the vessels of the temple they would go and build. What we take from contemporary fashion is flawed both in matter and in form. There is no way to elevate things like yoga pants, skinny jeans, and hoodies to the noble beauty that clothing can and should possess. Normalcy students wave dismissively at modesty as a state of mind, and, while they wish to promote beauty, they tend to hold such relativistic views of it that their dress rarely reflects anything more than the prevailing zeitgeist. Clothing today, unlike in previous eras, does not point to higher truth: one's identity as a man or a woman, as a member of a particular land, as a participant in a particular art or craft or social role. Rather, today's clothing only reflects the dehumanizing and ultimately diabolical power of industrialism, utilitarianism, rationalism, feminism, and gender ideology. These evils all have their DNA embedded in the fashions of today. Those who wear them, like it or not, spread their messages. On the dangers of the insidious spirit of the times, Dietrich von Hildebrand issues an urgent warning:

> This zeitgeist of the industrialized world is itself a lie. It contradicts the true, genuine, valid rhythm of human life, a rhythm that is indissolubly linked to the objective essence of the poetry of human life. We must fight this zeitgeist and redeem man from this curse.[1]

Those Catholics who attempt to adapt themselves and their dress to a world that values comfort as a virtue and imposes drab mediocrity on every man, woman, and child inadvertently reinforce the curse.

How, then, do we dress? Given that dress is indeed an art and the theme of art is beauty, an obvious solution surfaces: we must

---

[1] Dietrich von Hildebrand, *Aesthetics* (Hildebrand Project, 2018), vol. 2, p. 65.

enroll first and foremost in the school of our predecessors, the School of Beauty.[2] This is not to say that we must make exact replicas of historical dress, but, if we are to restore beauty to dress, we must study those who have done it before and done it amazingly well. What was handed down to them as naturally as the languages they spoke, we must, like feeble patients recovering from a stroke, begin the slow and difficult work of rehabilitating. Catholic artists, philosophers, historians, and writers must take up hard questions without bowing to specious arguments for "states of mind" and "cultural norms." What actually constitutes beautiful dress? What ways of dress are best for the salvation of man? And what must we do to begin?

Despite the enormity of the challenge, hope prevails. After all, two pillars of the triad that must support the art of dress are already in place: with the Church's teaching on the Incarnation, the differences and complementarity of the sexes, and the ultimate purpose of each human life, we see that the *pillar of truth* already stands firm. Furthermore, the Church's clear teachings on the necessity of chastity, modesty, and fraternal charity form the *pillar of goodness*. It is now only the third pillar, the one of beauty, that is lacking, thus causing the triad to topple sideways.[3] But this need not be the case. We Catholics, sons and daughters of the most beautiful cultural heritage the world has ever produced, need not be content to dress in an ugly, impoverished way. The time to begin the rehabilitation is long past due, and though we depend on guidance from artists and intellectuals of good taste, we all, as daily practitioners of the art of dress, bear tremendous responsibility.

Let us begin.

---

[2] Hildebrand, 2:47.
[3] I owe the triad formula to Dr. Peter Kwasniewski who shared it with me in correspondence.

2

Problems with Normalcy

IN THE PREVIOUS CHAPTER, I REMINDED readers that dress is an art, and I hinted that there are certain artistic principles which should govern this art. That is, from an aesthetical point of view, there are right and wrong ways of dressing. However, before delving into these principles, which are fascinating and rewarding, I would like first to explore more deeply the notion of normalcy. I would like my readers to understand that the "normal" fashions of today do not follow, but rather flout, artistic principles. Fashion designers today, be they designing for the runway or the racks of Walmart, do not want men and women to look beautiful.

In this chapter, I underscore how untenable this line of thinking I call the School of Normalcy is for the restoration of truly beautiful dress and why "just looking normal," pleasant as the idea may seem, is a strategy that ultimately bears no fruit.

As I noted in the last chapter, the School of Normalcy is a school of thought that promotes "normal" or "relevant" modes of dress on the grounds that (1) these modes can be worthy and attractive and (2) they will help to integrate their wearers into modern society for the better glorification of God. This school's adherents are usually conservative Catholics who, on the one hand, understand the profound significance of clothing, but who, on the other hand, cling to the notion that they can be modern and integrated rather than frumpy, prudish, or just plain odd like some of their Catholic brethren. Clad in hoodies and jeans, drab pants suits, or strappy sundresses, they see themselves as undercover agents expertly disseminating the Faith in universities, the office, and Starbucks.

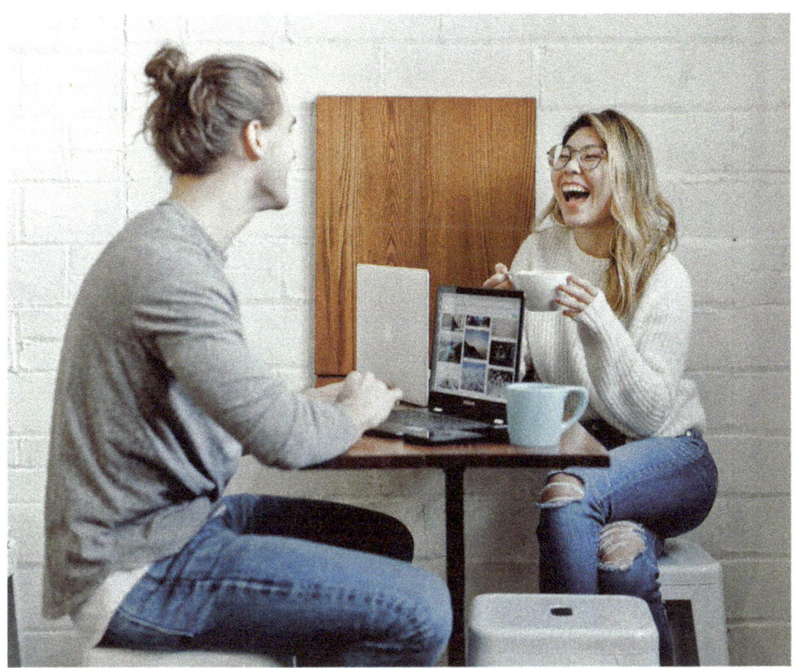

Figure 1. Man and woman in "normal" dress: thoroughly relevant and setting the world on fire ... or they think so anyway. (PHOTO: BROOKE CAGLE)

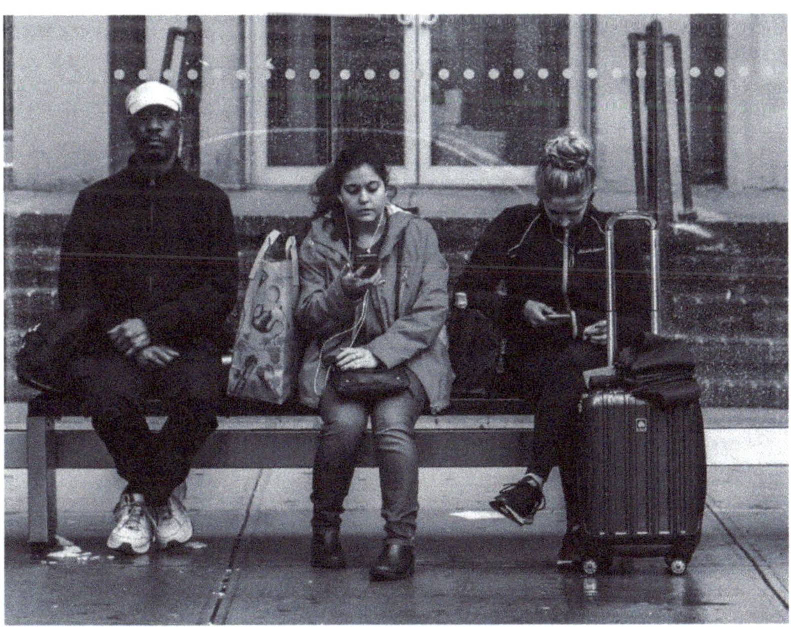

Figure 2. Another example of normal dress: dull, utilitarian, bleak.
(PHOTO: CRAIG ADDERLEY)

Normalcy advocates argue that their approach differs little from that of the saints throughout history who have embraced contemporaneous modes of dress and saved souls along the way: Louis IX looked like a medieval king, Margaret Clitherow like an Elizabethan housewife, Thérèse (pre-Carmel) like a daughter of the Belle Époque's petite bourgeoisie, and so on. They all became saints, the School of Normalcy's disciples point out; we may do the same.

On the surface, this approach seems fairly reasonable. However, underneath its appealing façade, it hides some imposing problems.

First, the School of Normalcy is not historically accurate. It implicitly holds that, with regard to dress, one period's fashions are worth the same as the next; whether one likes certain fashions more than others is entirely a matter of taste. The school will readily admit that our ancestors dressed differently, but far be it from them to hint that our ancestors dressed better. Normalcy's adherents do not acknowledge that we do not exist on the same historical continuum as most of the saints they hold as models. There has been, in fact, a distinct rupture that has dislodged every art today from that continuum.

Even secular commentators acknowledge what this school refuses to see, namely, that an enormous cultural rupture took place around the time of the First World War. This rupture had a devastating impact on all of the arts. In a *Los Angeles Times* article, Reed Johnson describes the cultural landscape as follows:

> During and after World War I, flowery Victorian language was blown apart and replaced by more sinewy and R-rated prose styles. In visual art, Surrealists and Expressionists devised wobbly, chopped-up perspectives and nightmarish visions of fractured human bodies and splintered societies slouching toward moral chaos.... Cynicism toward the ruling classes and disgust with war planners and profiteers led to demands for art forms that were honest and direct, less embroidered with rhetoric and euphemism.[1]

---

[1] Reed Johnson, "Art forever changed by World War I," *Los Angeles Times*, July 21, 2012.

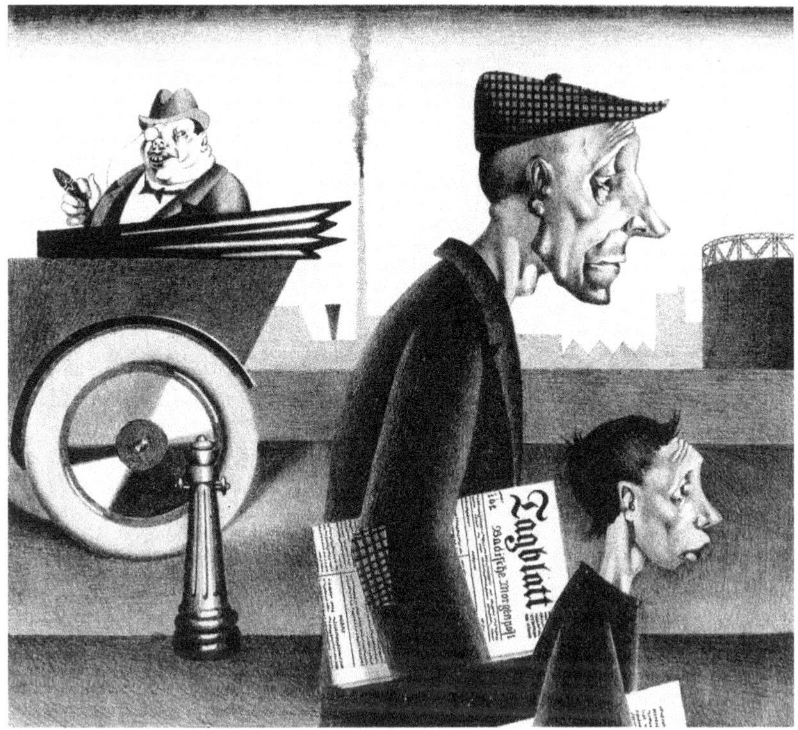

Figure 3. Art after the rupture: Georg Scholz,
"Newspaper Carriers (Work Disgraces)," 1921

With this cynicism came profound scorn for all that was deemed romantic, sentimental, and frivolous. Utility was God.

Applied arts such as dress were no longer recognized as arts at all, with the emphasis on wartime utility stifling all thought of aesthetic value. Historian Hannah Stamler writes, "in a brief span of four years, women's fashion went from frivolous to functional."[2] Her observation highlights at once the drastic change that took place in women's dress and the prevailing bias held by contemporary historians such as herself—namely, that ornamented, less "functional" dress is merely frivolous or even, as many claim, oppressive and begging for radical change.

[2] Hannah Stamler, "In Pictures: How World War I Changed Women's Fashion," *Frieze,* November 19, 2019.

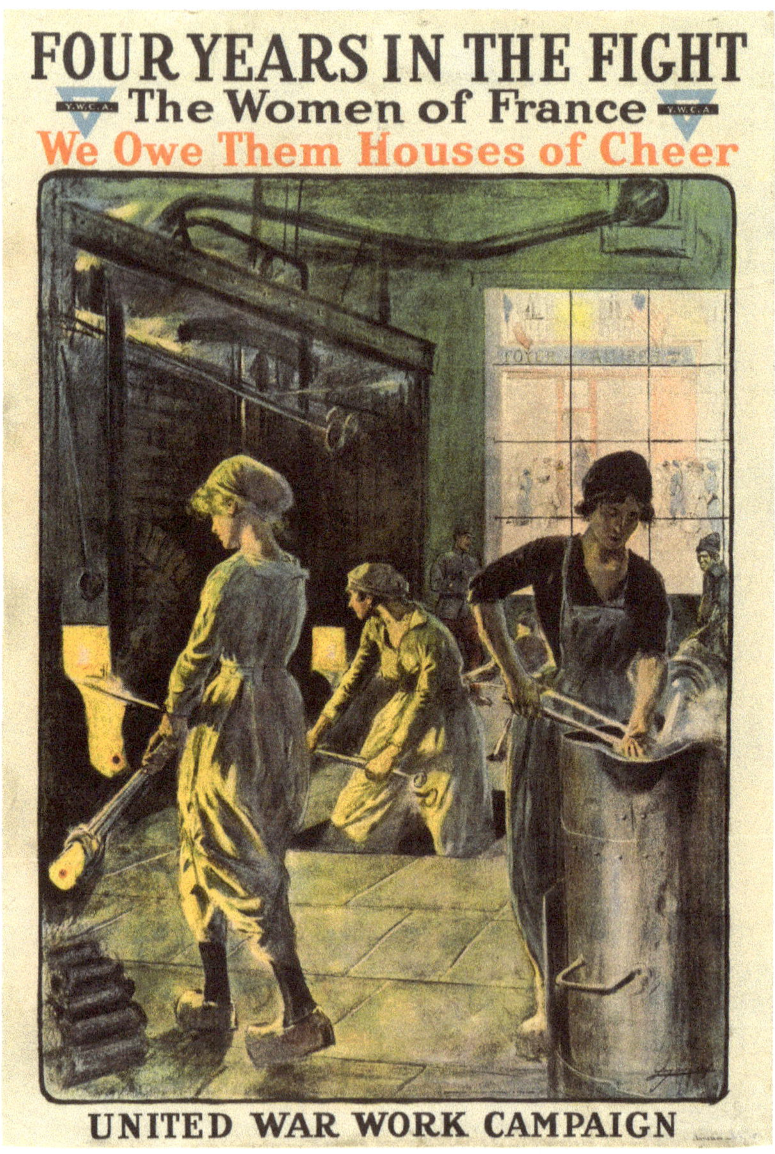

Figure 4. Women dressed for factory work during World War I.
(SOURCE: NATIONAL WWI MUSEUM AND MEMORIAL)

Now, some may point to particular sartorial successes which followed the world wars—for instance, stunning costumes of Hollywood or the everyday elegance of white gloves and pillbox hats—but these were not so much a revitalization of dress as wistful echoes of better days. The drastic changes to dress that spewed forth from the Sexual Revolution in the sixties were merely the aftershock of something that had begun much earlier.[3]

In his *Aesthetics*, Dietrich von Hildebrand places the moment of rupture several decades prior to the Great War:

> Until the beginning of the nineteenth century and the triumph of the machine, culture had not yet been strangled by civilization. The expression of the spirit, the gift of giving form in such a way that was not practically indispensable, penetrated all the practical spheres of life up to that time. A knife should not only cut well; it should also possess a noble form. A chair should not only be comfortable and solid; it should also be beautiful, in fact it should sooner be a little less comfortable than be sober and prosaic. Practical life as a whole possessed an organic character and was therefore united to a special poetry of life. Related to this was the penetration of life by culture. But as the practical life of the human being was robbed of its organic character and was mechanized and thereby depersonalized, so too the poetry of practical life was lost.[4]

As an illustration of these words, one might think of Tolkien's idyllic shire, peopled by those who "did not understand or like machines more complicated than a forge-bellows, a water-mill, or a hand-loom," versus the hellish city of Isengard controlled by Saruman's "mind of metal and wheels."[5]

With these considerations, should we not pause before adopting the modes of a civilization that has strangled culture? Can we, like the School of Normalcy, turn a blind eye to historical fact and pretend as if the art of dress has ambled along the avenues of time unscathed by post-Industrial ideologies? Would the saints who have gone before us, the ones who chopped down the Druids' trees and overturned pagan altars, actually have recommended this approach? The School of Normalcy never acknowledges these questions, much less answers them.

---

3 Linda Przybyszewski, *The Lost Art of Dress* (Basic Books, 2014), 191–92.
4 Hildebrand, *Aesthetics*, 2:52.
5 J.R.R. Tolkien, *The Lord of the Rings* (Houghton Mifflin Company, 1994), 1:1 and 2:462.

The next problem with the School of Normalcy is its failure to recognize beauty as an objective and crucial component in the art of dress. With scores of cloying platitudes, its proponents assure women that *they* are beautiful inside and out, and so they must simply discover their "personal style" to live as integrated, authentic Catholic women. One may search countless blogs and turn the pages of several recently published books and still come away uncertain of what actually constitutes beautiful dress.

Of course women are beautiful. All humans, even apparently homely ones, have beauty by means of their ontological dignity and, if they are virtuous, by means of their holiness. But this notwithstanding, the domain of beauty that actually pertains to the art of dress is, to our limited human perception, another thing altogether.[6]

Ontological and spiritual beauty do not guarantee visible beauty. A person with a beautiful soul may have a homely face and wear ugly clothing. However, it is certainly fitting and right that the children of God seek to wear visibly beautiful clothing not only as a sign of respect for their bodies (homely or not), but as a wordless way to speak of and be in harmony with their invisible beauties. It is, presumably, the duty of Catholic writers on dress to guide their readers to beautiful clothing with instruction grounded on aesthetical principles and a true philosophical understanding of beauty. Unfortunately, the School of Normalcy possesses no such principles or understanding.

Returning to historical considerations, I would like to point out the amazing intuition that guided our ancestors (mostly poor and illiterate) to produce truly beautiful clothing. With relatively little talk of aesthetics, they somehow managed to produce wonderful works of art in all fields, not the least dress. From the charm of peasant dress to the stunning achievements of Renaissance textiles, it would seem that the air they breathed fueled the growth of the art of dress. For all of their wars, famines, plagues, and scarcity, a guiding force silently elevated their dress in a way that we, in the era of comfort, utility, and mass-production can hardly fathom.

---

[6] Hildebrand, *Aesthetics*, 1:75–101.

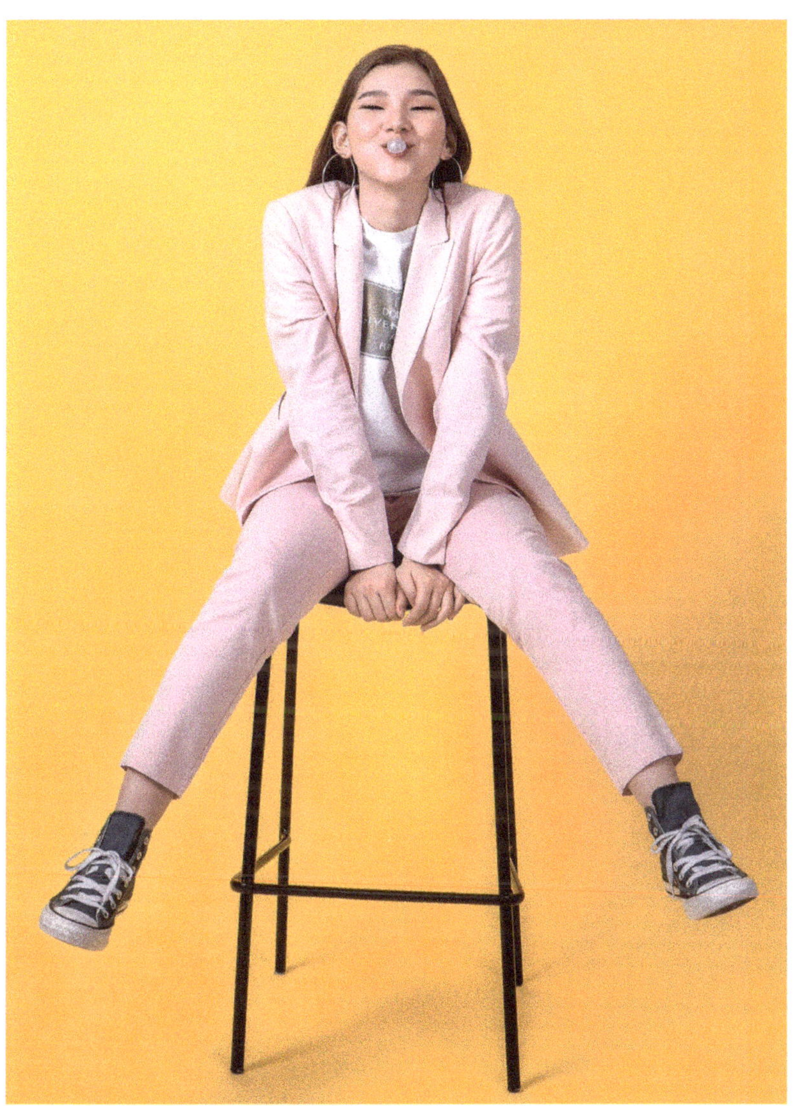

Figure 5. What the world calls "personal expression":
the School of Normalcy would celebrate this girl's
"sporty, personal style." (PHOTO: MIKOTO.RAW)

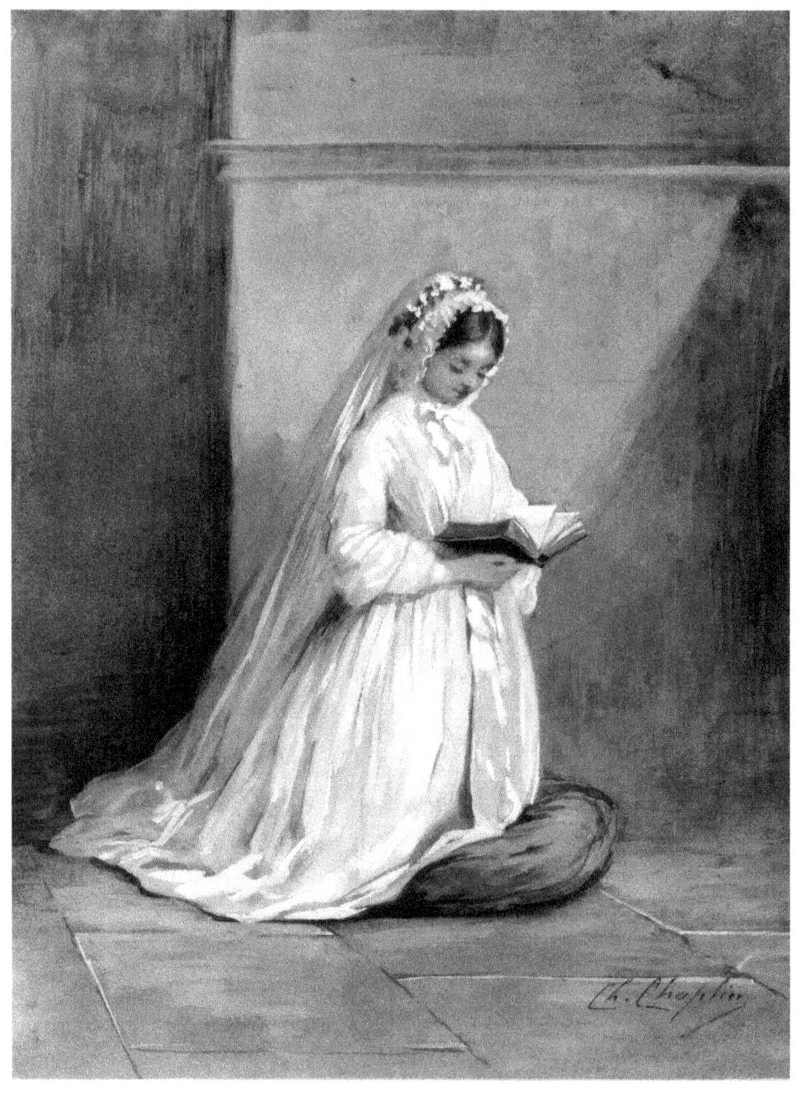

Figure 6. A sacramental gown, far different from today's norm: Charles Joshua Chaplin, "Girl in Confirmation Dress at Prayer," 1860.

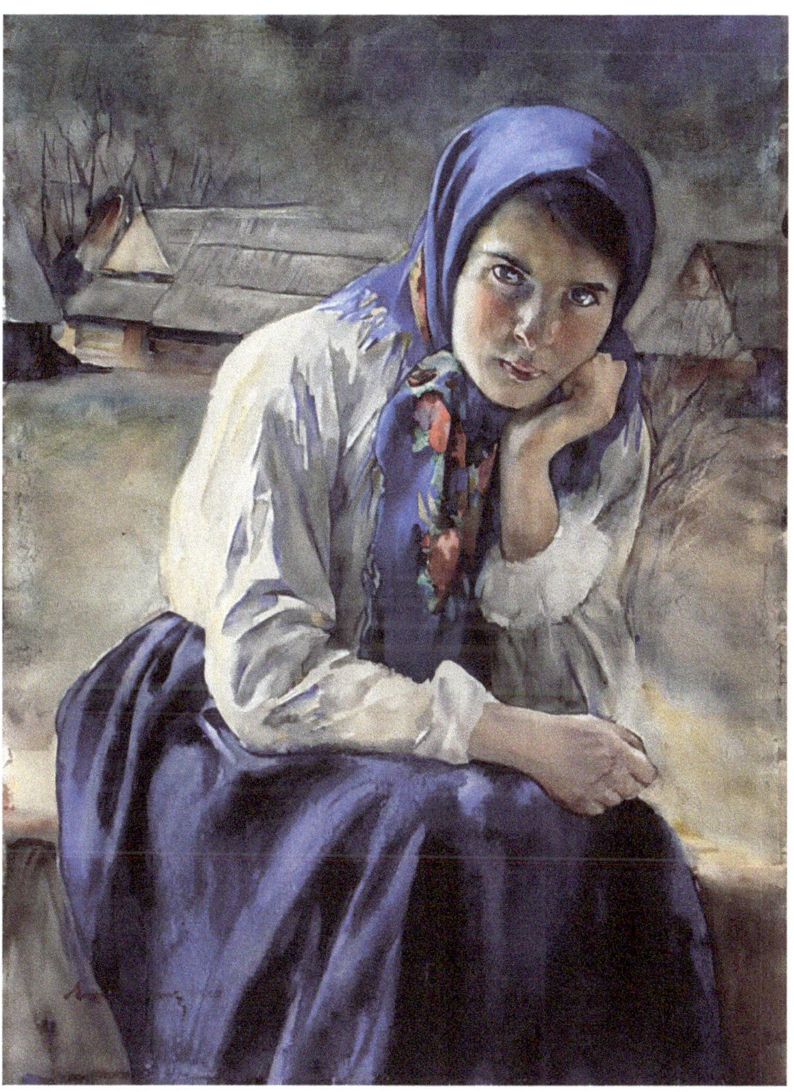

Figure 7. Beauty and simplicity in Polish peasant dress:
Aleksander Augustynowicz, "Portrait of a Girl
in Traditional Costume," 1916.

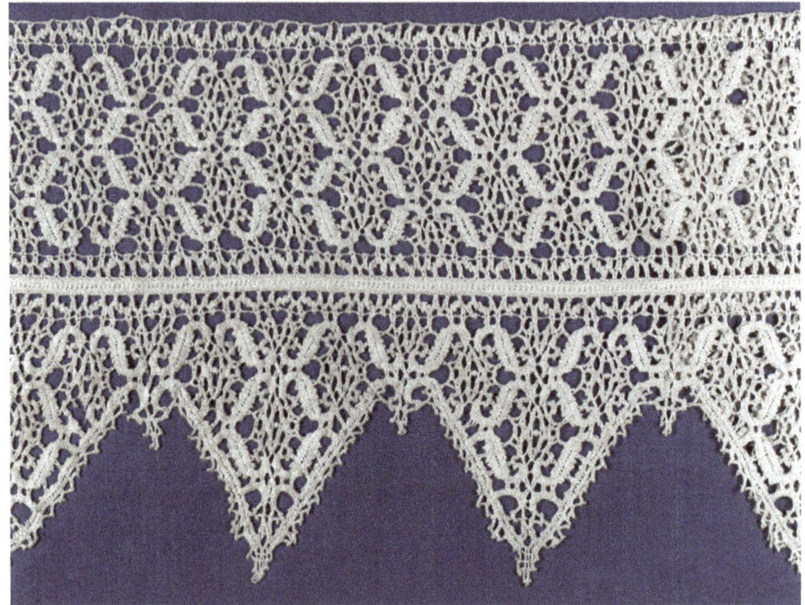

Figure 8. Hand-made Italian lace. (SOURCE: METROPOLITAN MUSEUM OF ART)

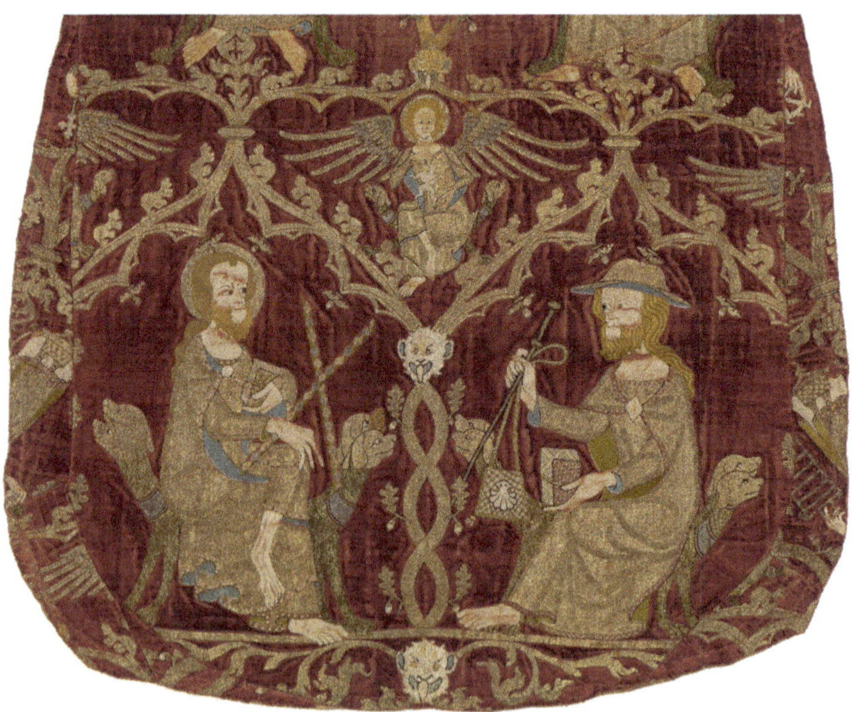

Figure 9. The lower portion of the back of a medieval
chasuble. (SOURCE: METROPOLITAN MUSEUM OF ART)

For us today, dress is not an art that grows up organically from the homes and small towns of Christendom. Rather, it hurtles down on us from the ideological towers of nameless oligarchs. We seem to have no choice but to accept formless, "gender-neutral" cuts, sloppy wrinkle-proof ease, tawdry prints, and sensual second-skin loungewear. One may see this attire on full display not only in any airport, sports venue, or gas station, but in most restaurants, schools, and churches as well. Furthermore, in an entirely new phenomenon, the very wealthy often appear ugliest of all. It is a kind of mass aesthetical perversion.

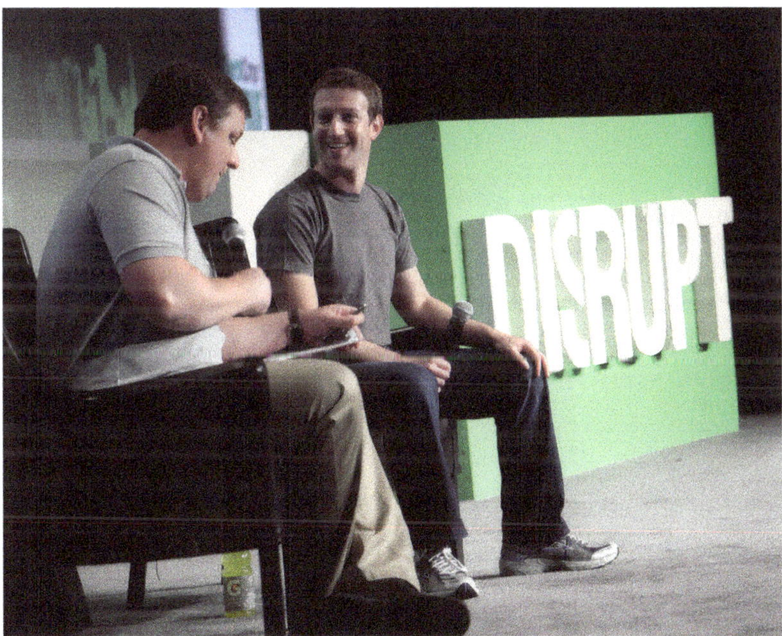

Figure 10. The elite dressed poorly: drab, prosaic clothes for one of the wealthiest men in the world. (PHOTO: TECHCRUNCH)

As beings made in the image and likeness of God, we must seek to reflect the all-beautiful God. Men and women arrayed in ugly clothing (even with the best intentions) generate an illusion, an obstruction to the truth about who we are, which can only harm souls and thwart evangelization.

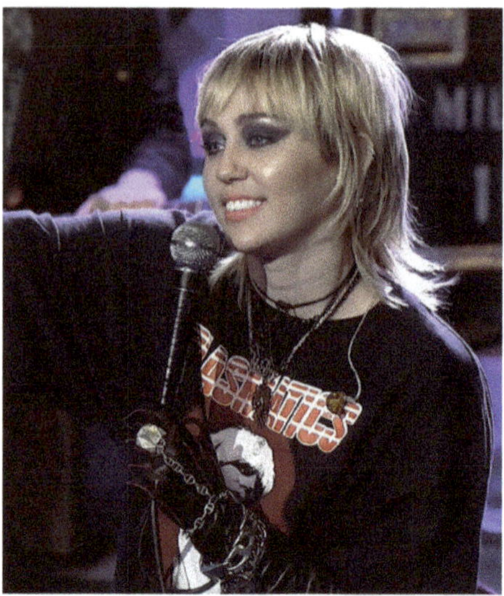

Figure 11. The elite wallowing in ugliness: she could have worn anything money could buy—and she chose this. (PHOTO: AZRAULKER)

One may still pause to ask why, if beauty in dress is so desirable and its lack so deplorable, more Catholics do not awaken to the flaws of contemporary dress. Indeed, it seems that even the most devout Catholics take no offense at the absence of beauty in their attire and hold little longing for any improvement. Dietrich von Hildebrand comments on this perplexing atrophy of aesthetic sensitivity:

> People have grown accustomed to the elimination of the poetry of the world, to the mechanization of life, to the expulsion of beauty; but this does not make any less real the influence on human happiness of this destruction of the charm of an organic, truly human life.[7]

Given the ubiquity of clothing—after all, every man, woman, and child must dress daily—is it not very likely that the ugliness of our clothes contributes in a great measure to the malaise of our present day? The School of Normalcy's failure to acknowledge the lack of beauty in contemporary dress, and its students' apparent oblivious-ness to this omission, only proves how dire the situation has become.

[7] Hildebrand, 1:4.

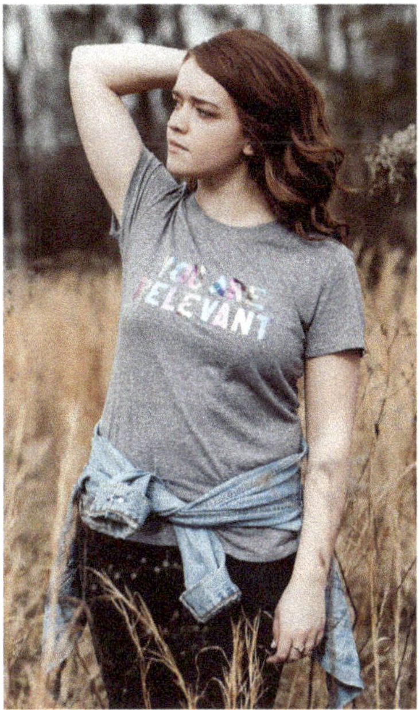

Figure 12. So-called "relevant" dress. Today, appearing "relevant" actually means donning bland, ugly clothing at odds with human beauty and the beauty of creation. (PHOTO: BROOKE CAGLE)

But surely, one may interject, the greatest source of the School of Normalcy's appeal among well-meaning Catholics is not so much a desire to fit in, and still less a desire to give up on beauty, but rather a desire to simply come to peace with the conditions into which God has placed us. After all, we were born in *this* era, and we have to wear *something*.

These are valid points. The problem arises when the desire for peace turns into a blind promotion of modernity and relevance, as if these pseudo-virtues are actual spiritual goods, and as if our era is not markedly different from previous ones. This desperate clinging to a strategy founded on fallacies denies the urgent duty to fight against the destructive spirit of our age that would make the world ever more hideous.[8] The saints we hold as models clung

---

[8] Hildebrand, 2:65–66. Here, Hildebrand emphasizes the urgent educational task of architecture, and one can easily see the same ideas applied to dress. "Architecture is not only an expression of a living cultural world. It also has

to the good, the true, and the beautiful. We must do the same.

Undeniably, we all have to bear with contemporary dress to one degree or another, but we must recognize that we are bearing with and not embracing and, in doing so, are positioning ourselves to jump on every opportunity to improve matters. It is not vanity or snobbishness to hold that we do not dress as we ought and to go out of our way for better clothing when we can. It is sanity. If we never admit that we have taken a wrong road, we will never turn and find the right road.[9]

While we will not likely see the beauty of medieval court dress, or the charm of traditional folk costumes, or even the relatively subdued elegance of the Edwardians restored in our lifetime, we may still plant seeds for a restoration in subsequent generations. This does not mean that we should cherry-pick one "perfect" mode from history and seek to re-create that. In a discussion of architecture that applies equally well to the art of dress, Hildebrand sheds light on the question as follows:

> It is indeed meaningful to say that the architect should not imitate any style of earlier periods. But at the same time, we must explicitly emphasize that the true artist should pay no heed at all to the zeitgeist. He should create a building in which the general artistic requirements are fully satisfied. He can employ many motifs, including those from earlier periods, but these will be inserted completely into the special invention of the specific building.[10]

With regard to dress, we need not make ourselves historical reenactors, but we must certainly learn from our forebears. We *can* and

the eminent educational task today of liberating the zeitgeist from its barren depoeticization and mechanization. . . . This is why the task for contemporary architecture is very different from that in epochs in which the poetry of life still developed without hindrance and a rich cultural world filled their inner space. Today architecture must fight against the zeitgeist, not through imitation of older styles, but through the unchecked use of great architectural inventions of the past, in order to create something new that is nourished by the artistic inspiration of the architect—but not by the zeitgeist."

9 C. S. Lewis, *Mere Christianity* (HarperCollins, 2001), 28–29.

10 Hildebrand, *Aesthetics*, 2:65.

should seek quality over quantity, embrace greater formality, and prioritize tasteful ornamentation over utility.[11]

We must remember that dress is an art and true art grows organically.[12] This reality, rather than daunting us, should actually bring us peace—and patience. Living as we do in a kind of cultural ground zero, our primary task is to clear rubble (e.g., get rid of ugly clothes) and cultivate soil for future growth.

Cultivating involves an entire re-evaluation of our way of life. First, we should ask ourselves how we worship God. Is the liturgy we attend a source of beauty that draws us up to God and reveals His majesty? Is it something that can, from its supreme height, trickle down through every aspect of our lives? Or is it a horizontal plane on which we can see nothing but ourselves and the drab gray of our own exile?

And do we have time for leisure in which we might embrace our God-given creativity, that quality that sets us apart from all other creatures and sets us so amazingly close to Him? Or do we fill our time with the cheap distractions of television and social media? If we don't know how to make a simple greeting card for a friend or arrange a small vase of flowers, it's unlikely we'll ever learn much about how to satisfy the general artistic requirements of dress.

We must, above all, be ready to sacrifice. The work of restoration is a daily cross and a stripping away of ease, of comfort, and of the consolation of having a "normal" life. Yet it will bring a new richness: our God is generous, and He will not despise our efforts. As sacred artist Gwyneth Thompson-Briggs puts it: "Any time I've consented to pick up a cross of beauty and carry it, the sacrifice has expanded my love and brought great joy."[13] May we now and always pick up our crosses of beauty and follow Our Lord, the source of all love and joy.

---

[11] See chapters 3 and 4.
[12] Hildebrand, *Aesthetics*, 2:8–9.
[13] Fr. Michael Rennier, quoting Gwyneth Thompson-Briggs: "Starting today, here's how to make your life more beautiful," *Aleteia*, February 20, 2022.

3

Art Principles

I HAVE MADE PASSING REFERENCES TO ART principles in previous chapters. Let us now consider them at length.

In 1925, professors of home economics Harriet and Vetta Goldstein published a textbook called *Art in Everyday Life*. The book and its three subsequent editions soon become a key reference for virtually all other textbooks on dress of the time and ended up influencing generations of American homemakers.[1]

The sisters began the book with an introduction to good taste in their distinctly simple prose:

> It has been said that good taste is doing unconsciously the right thing, at the right time, in the right way. Unfortunately, very few people are born with this rare gift, but it is comforting to know that with study one can consciously apply the principles, until the wished for time is reached when the right thing is done unconsciously.[2]

They then presented their formulation of art principles: Harmony, Proportion, Balance, Rhythm, and Emphasis. In subsequent chapters, they covered topics as varied as hat selection, interior design, and city planning—their principles applied to all.[3]

With occasional references to "the Greeks" and Japanese prints as their authorities, the Goldsteins took for granted in their students a desire for beauty and a willingness to bow to universal

---

[1] Przybyszewski, *Lost Art of Dress*, 17–18.
[2] Harriet and Vetta Goldstein, *Art in Everyday Life* (MacMillan Company, 1930), 3.
[3] Goldstein, 5.

principles.[4] Commenting, for instance, on texture harmony, it was enough to say:

> In dress we sometimes see textures as inharmonious
> as gold-lace hats worn with coarse wool sweaters, and
> strings of pearls with rough wool dresses. The gold-lace
> hat and pearls are related, and are harmonious in texture
> with such fabrics as satin, velvet, and fine furs. The wool
> sweater and the wool dress have textures which would be
> in harmony with each other and with felt, rough straw,
> or similar textures.[5]

This clear guidance contrasts drastically with that found in the digital maelstrom of today's fashion commentary, which seems to value comfort above all and which treats aesthetic value—whatever it asserts that might be—only as a means to shock or seduce.

The Goldstein sisters' challenge to their students to bring beauty to every sphere of life, and their candid avowal that one must follow *rules* to do so, would make their book seem thoroughly "biased" to the intelligentsia of today. And yet, among the general population, there are many who, marveling at the beauty of Grace Kelly's wedding dress, or their own great grandmother's attire in a faded family photo, begin to suspect that, to reclaim some portion of what they admire, it might just be worthwhile to study something with more backbone than the latest vapid fashion blog.

I will now present a brief survey of the Goldsteins' work regarding the art of dress to show how it might guide us today. I write particularly for women who, struggling to dress modestly, have run up against inevitable frumpiness, who wonder wistfully why even their poorest ancestors looked so much better than they, and who wish to make of dress something more than a dreary duty. In short, this survey of art principles is for the benefit of women who believe that dress can and should be a source of great joy.

---

[4] Przybyszewski, *Lost Art of Dress*, 65–66 and 53, and Goldstein, *Art in Everyday Life*, ch. 4.
[5] Goldstein, 49.

HARMONY

When we think of harmony, our thoughts likely go first to music. But taken in a broader sense, harmony is merely the successful arrangement of things, be they musical notes, buildings, or bracelets. Harmony and disharmony occur in all realms of art.

The Goldsteins describe harmony as "the art principle which produces an impression of unity through the selection and arrangement of consistent objects and ideas."[6] They describe harmonious objects and ideas as having "family resemblances" and "friendly" relationships with one another, and they break harmony into four sub-categories: shape, texture, idea, and color.[7]

Shape harmony

Regarding shape harmony in dress, the Goldsteins offer the following instruction:

> Since a dress design in itself is not considered as a complete unit, but as something to be worn on a human figure, its lines should suggest some relationship to the lines of the figure. This means that its outline will follow the form closely enough to have something in common with it, yet not so closely as to appear immodest or to be uncomfortable.[8]

One finds here a refreshingly balanced perspective of the shape question so often considered only from the angle of how much ought to be hidden. A *human* wears the clothes; therefore, it is proper and logical to show some suggestion of the *human* shape rather than to obscure it completely in the name of modesty. In warning against the other extreme, that is, clingy clothing, the Goldsteins assume their readers not only know what modesty is, but also desire it. Not prone to philosophizing or preaching, perhaps they found the admonishment to ease of motion an easier one to support. Besides, in their day, stretch fabrics had not yet made second-skin leggings and tank tops a possibility, so anyone looking for ease of motion would have necessarily worn looser-fitting clothing. In the section on emphasis, I will further discuss the problems with clingy clothing.

---

[6] Goldstein, 21.   [7] Goldstein, 21–56.   [8] Goldstein, 36–37.

To further understand shape harmony, consider the figures below:

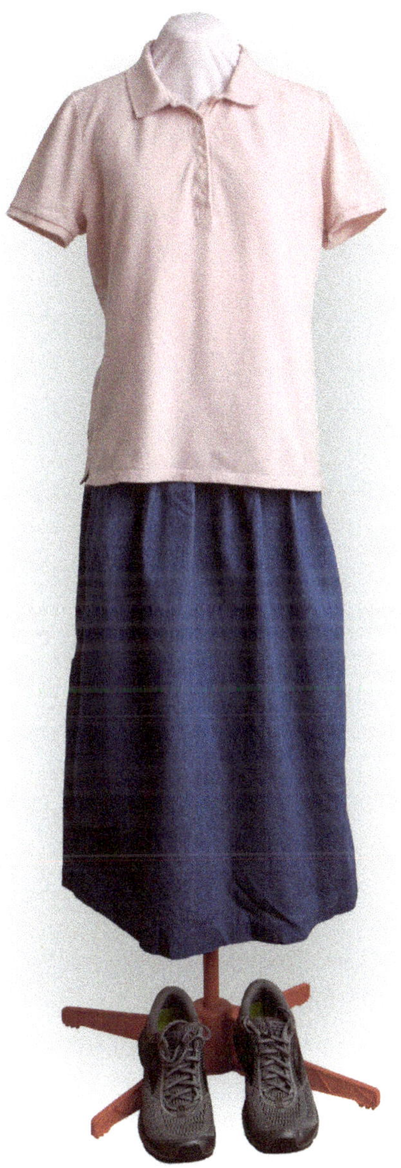

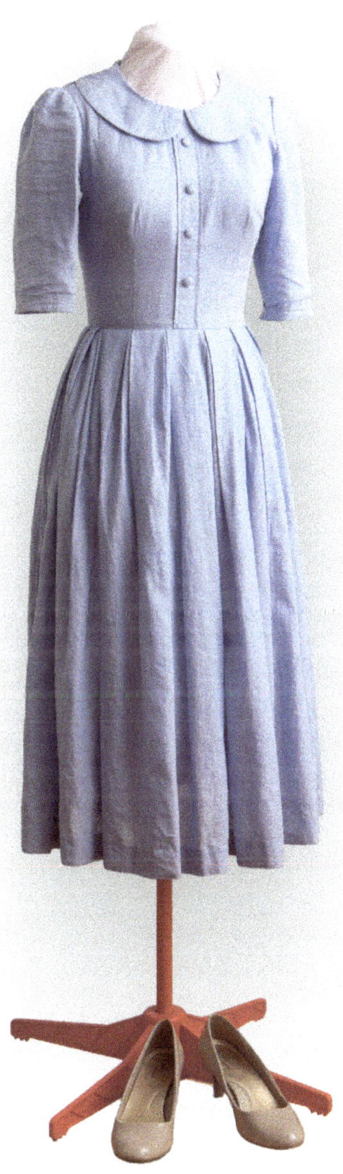

Figure 1. Lack of shape harmony: clothing not in harmony with the human figure.

(PHOTO: CAMERON MCCARTY)

Figure 2. Successful shape harmony: clothing in harmony with the human figure.

(PHOTO: CAMERON MCCARTY)

Although the ensemble in Figure 1 succeeds in decently covering the wearer, it shows very little shape harmony. The baggy, untucked polo shirt obscures the figure beneath. The skirt fails to fall gracefully over the hips and instead seems to hang midair in a stiff wad. The shoes do not allow the figure to taper at the feet, but, rather, they stand out like two heavy blobs. This ensemble, though less than ideal, could be greatly improved simply by tucking in the shirt (assuming the skirt sits at the natural waist) and exchanging the sneakers for light flats or sandals.

The dress in Figure 2 also succeeds in decently covering the wearer, but this time it shows successful shape harmony. The bodice, though fitted, does not cling. Its seam, at the natural waist, harmonizes perfectly with the wearer beneath. The ordered gathers of the skirt fall gracefully over the hips, at once concealing and revealing the beauty of the figure. It is worth noting, too, that the gentle puffs at the shoulders provide ease of motion remarkable for a fabric (a cotton-linen blend) with no stretch. The length of the sleeves and their narrowing down to the elbow harmonizes better with the arm of the wearer than the gaping quarter-length sleeves of the standard polo shirt in Figure 1.

While this contrasting pair of figures is just one example, the points mentioned in this analysis can assist one in evaluating many kinds of ensembles, and one can gain greater aptitude for creating shape harmony simply from this awareness: that we must seek clothing that is in harmony with the human figure.

Texture harmony

On harmony of textures, the Goldsteins underscore a great secret to artistic success: namely, that materials exist in roughly three texture families—coarse, fine, and transitional—and that, to achieve harmony in a design, all materials used must originate (or seem to originate) from the same family. For instance, the common durability and weight of denim, rough wool, and leathers such as rawhide makes them siblings. Just as one expects to see the brothers and sisters of a family together, so it appears natural for related materials to comprise an ensemble of clothing. In the realm of fine materials, the similar luster of pearls and satin makes them like two radiant sisters, and one could call lace their cheerful cousin. Straw and light fabrics such as muslin and linen share a common summer airiness. Fur, wool, and velvet share a soft, quiet warmth akin to the gentle calm of a snowy night. And so on. It is beyond the scope of this survey to determine what generates family relationships of materials—are they only a human association, or something metaphysical? Here it suffices to repeat the Goldsteins' simple statement: "So many schemes just miss being successful because the person who planned them did not recognize that textures which are very coarse have nothing in common with those which are very fine."[9]

Ironically, most adherents of mainstream fashion accidentally achieve texture harmony simply because they never attempt anything beyond the most informal level of dress. Their T-shirts, yoga pants, and running shoes all fall in the same family of what might be called "synthetic stretch" textures. Of course, this perpetual informality of the so-called athleisure style presents its own set of problems, but that is beyond the scope of this section.

Fairly often when devout Catholics endeavor to dress with formality, their texture schemes "just miss" for the very reason the Goldsteins state. For instance, the woman who pairs a light chiffon dress for Mass with a boxy unisex windbreaker produces disharmony. The utilitarian sport fabric and masculine shape of the one have nothing in common with the light fabric and femininity of the other. Nor do the shock-absorbing foam soles and neon mesh of sneakers have anything in common with a light cotton sundress. And perhaps the most ubiquitous and well-meant blunder of all: fine lace chapel veils have nothing in common with denim. Although most lace seen today is made of nylon and produced by machines (and therefore inexpensive), lace as a fabric family still enjoys an aura of great formality, even regality. Historically, lace was considered a precious fabric and counted as part of a kingdom's treasure. It will always clash with utility fabrics. Nor does it correct matters in the least to tie the chapel veil around the head do-rag style as one sometimes sees.

To further understand texture harmony, consider the following figures:

9 Goldstein, 48.

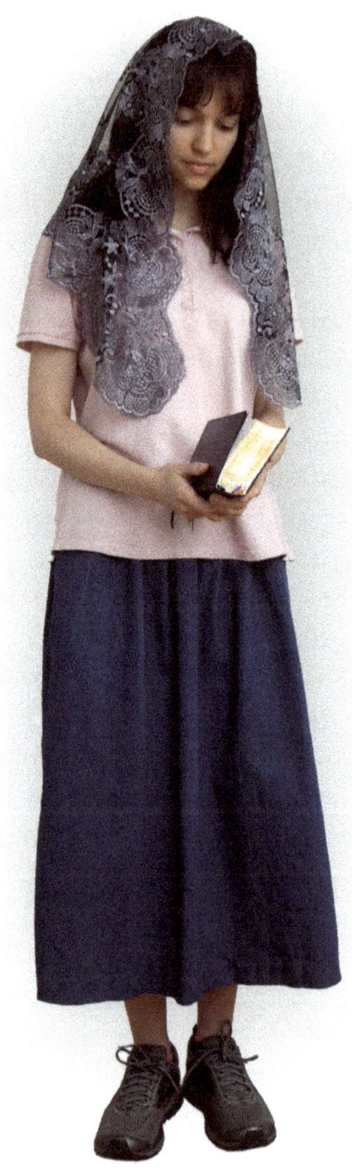

Figure 3. Lack of texture harmony: fine texture of lace does not harmonize with casual polo, denim, and running shoes. (PHOTO: CAMERON MCCARTY)

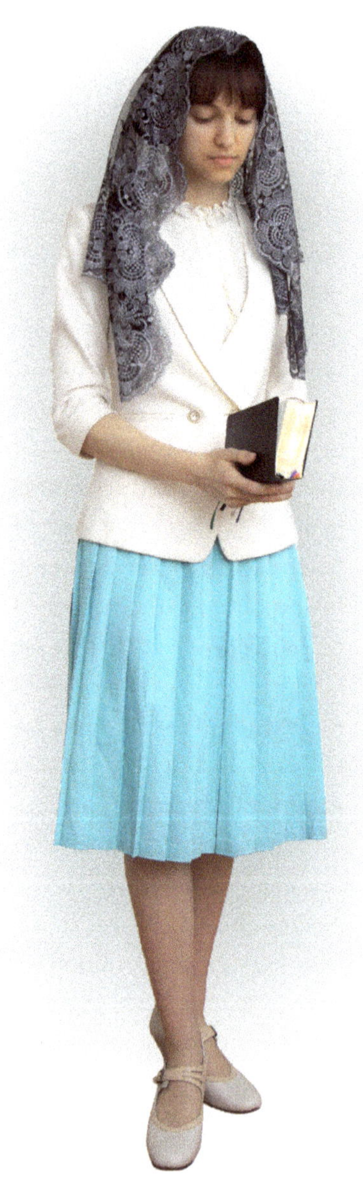

Figure 4. Successful texture harmony: fine texture of lace harmonizes with chiffon blouse, formal cut of blazer and skirt, and graceful shoes. (PHOTO: CAMERON MCCARTY)

Once again, while the figures show only one contrasting example, the important lesson is to begin thinking of the textures that appear in our ensembles. The more one thinks about the feel, the character, the appearance of a texture, the more one will begin to identify its sibling textures and thus create greater harmony in each ensemble.

In the Goldsteins' day, occurrences of disharmony were still largely the result of innocent artistic blunders and limitations in resources, as is the case among devout Catholics today. But in contemporary mainstream fashion, we see highly trained designers purposely generating ridiculous combinations such as combat boots paired with evening gowns or jeans with patent leather heels, and flaunting them before all the world. The forces which drive contemporary fashion subscribe to an ideology that dislikes beauty and therefore has no use for harmony. Contemporary designers call their creations "edgy," "fierce," or "tough," but these are meaningless labels used only to glamorize ugliness.[10]

Idea harmony

Art in Everyday Life introduces the important concept of idea harmony. "It is not enough that sizes, shapes, colors, and textures should have something in common," the Goldsteins write, "but there must be harmony in the ideas which are presented together."[11]

An ensemble of clothing may convey many ideas: the age of the wearer, the wearer's state in life, the wearer's present occupation, the time of year, etc. The more the ideas conveyed by an ensemble harmonize with one another, their wearer, and their surroundings, the more beauty the ensemble can achieve.

The light summer fabrics and brilliant colors (or dazzling whites) historically worn by those in tropical climates harmonize perfectly with their surroundings. These vivid hues seem to have grown out of their lush environment as a harmonious synthesis of nature's inspiration and human craft. On the other hand,

---

[10] Alexis Frawley and Jessica Glass, "Edgy Style: Fierce Fashion Tips to Level-Up Your Looks," *Stitch Fix*, June 14, 2022.
[11] Goldstein, *Art in Everyday Life*, 49.

the rich earth tones or warm jewel tones of fabrics historically used in colder climates harmonize well with the quiet sobriety of winter. A dress of flounces and polka dots clashes with the venerable dignity of an elderly woman but harmonizes well with the playful spirit of a child. Conversely, black lace and dark, heavy fabrics harmonize far better with a matron than with a little girl. Formal clothing cut in more restrictive styles and made of fine fabrics does not harmonize with occupations such as hiking or farming, which demand ease of motion and a kind of pragmatic kinship with the elements. On the other hand, the garbs of hiking and farming do not harmonize with ceremonies of high splendor such as liturgies, which point to things far above the mundane. These greatest occasions of life demand formal clothing in order to harmonize with the decorum and majesty of the prevailing atmosphere that has momentarily set aside life's various labors to bask in the divine.

One of the most common disharmonies found in the dress of devout Catholics comes from the disregard for seasonal dress. Velvet appears in July and hibiscus prints in January. The many devout women who amass collections of maxi skirts, those long tubes of striped or figured polyester, seem not to realize that the flimsy fabric and invariably garish summer prints will never look well with Eskimo boots.

Admittedly, wool and other winter-weight fabrics have become nearly impossible to obtain. Year-round, one can hardly find any-thing *but* thin, stretch polyester in loud prints. Nevertheless, the fact remains that the clash of ideas—summer and winter—creates disharmony. It is worth noting too that the change of seasons and the movements of the natural world in general have a profound impact on man's spirit. Dressing with a true consciousness of the seasons is a fundamental way to counteract forces which, through a glut of technology, seek to disconnect man from the natural world and the reflection of God therein.

To further understand idea harmony, consider the following figures:

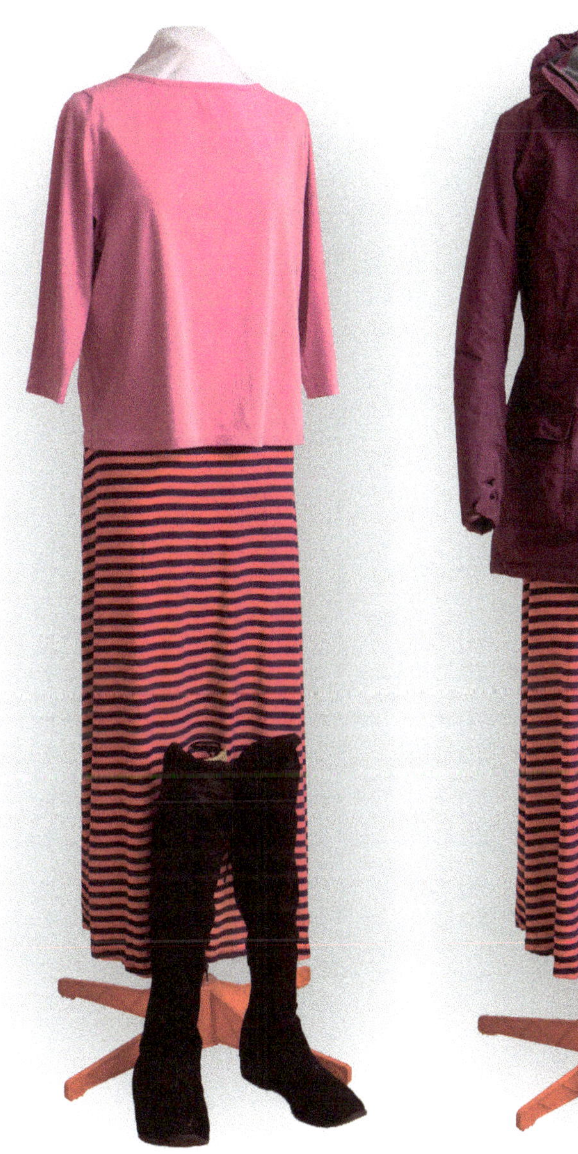

Figure 5. Inharmonious ideas: this skirt's thin fabric and nautical stripes lend themselves to summer, while the tall suede boots clearly belong in the autumn or winter.

(PHOTO: CAMERON MCCARTY)

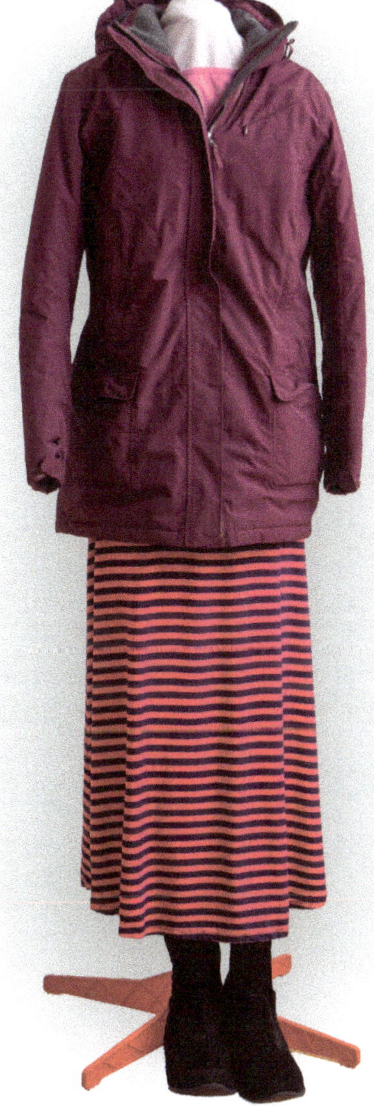

Figure 6. Inharmonious ideas: adding a bulky winter coat does not help matters.

(PHOTO: CAMERON MCCARTY)

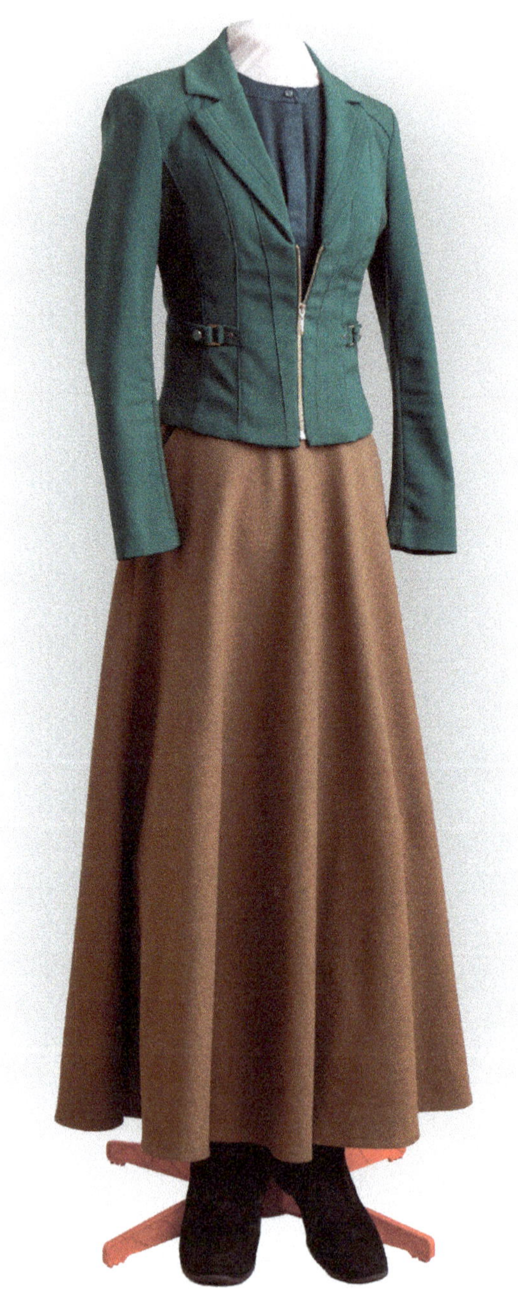

Figure 7. Successful idea harmony: here, the same boots as shown above harmonize with a wool skirt and autumnal color palette. (PHOTO: CAMERON MCCARTY)

Before concluding this discussion of idea harmony, one crucial point must be made. Although harmony with one's surroundings can very often result in great beauty, in the post-modern world one usually must draw a line of distinction as a kind of aesthetical pale that divides ordered beauty from the disordered chaos which surrounds us. For instance, a woman who must work every day in a Brutalist office building must not strive to harmonize with this ugliness. She must recognize that the architecture, furniture, and likely the dress of all those around her flows from an ideology that has rejected harmony and beauty. By dressing beautifully, she will, in fact, clash with her surroundings, but it is a clash that should occur, like a sounding bell in a sea of fog.

Color harmony

The fact that the Goldstein sisters devote two full chapters to an in-depth treatment of color theory in itself speaks of their disciplined approach to art. "In order to understand color and use it beautifully," they write, "it is necessary to learn enough color theory to understand color language and to know why one should choose certain colors rather than others."[12] They then go on to present both the Prang and Munsell color systems.

While it is beyond our present scope to retrace their steps here, for dress it is safe to say that the rules of traditional color theory apply, with the interesting additional challenge that the human figure represents not a blank white canvas but a complete work of art already. When dressing, one must consider how the colors of man's art (dress) play with those of God's art (the human complexion).

To further understand color harmony, consider the figures below.

The ensemble in Figure 8 possesses colors which are not inharmonious. Camel brown is light enough to pair with black without resulting in the discord one usually finds in black and brown combinations. However, with some knowledge of color theory, one may identify that camel brown is really a deep shade of orange; a quick glance at the color wheel and one sees that, to complement orange, one must use blue.

[12] Goldstein, 184.

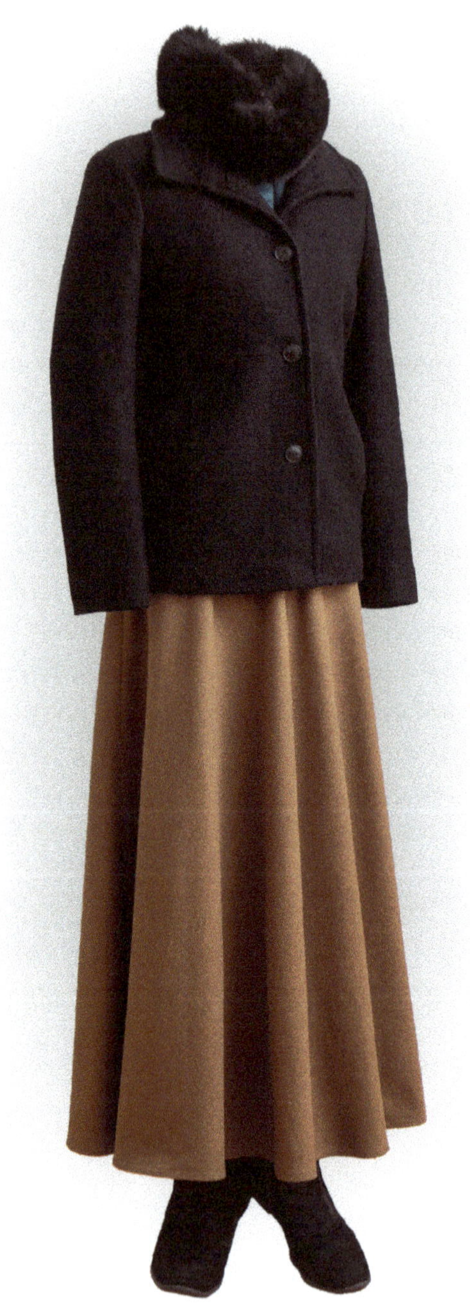

Figure 8. Adequate color harmony: camel brown and black look moderately well together. (PHOTO: CAMERON MCCARTY)

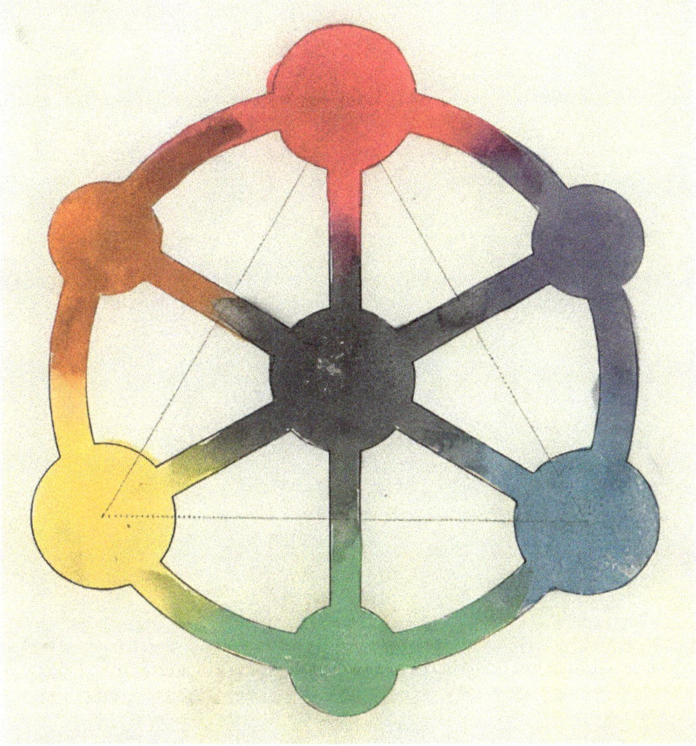

Figure 9. Mérimée color wheel. There are several color theory systems, but this simple color wheel, circa 1830, shows blue and orange opposite one another, indicating their complementarity. The darkening of each hue as it approaches the center of the color wheel shows the tendency of pigments to destroy each other upon being mixed. This is also called neutralization.

The trick is finding a blue with the same value (lightness or darkness) and intensity (level of neutrality) as the brown. Here, a navy blue suffices.

Figure 10 shows the classic navy blue and brown combination also exhibited by men who wear navy blue suits with brown shoes and belts. The human eye delights in this pairing because of the complementarity between the two colors. There are many other successful color schemes involving complements, other combinations, or subtle monochrome palettes. A study of traditional color theory, or even an awareness of its most basic tenets, will allow any practitioner of the art of dress to increase the beauty of every ensemble.

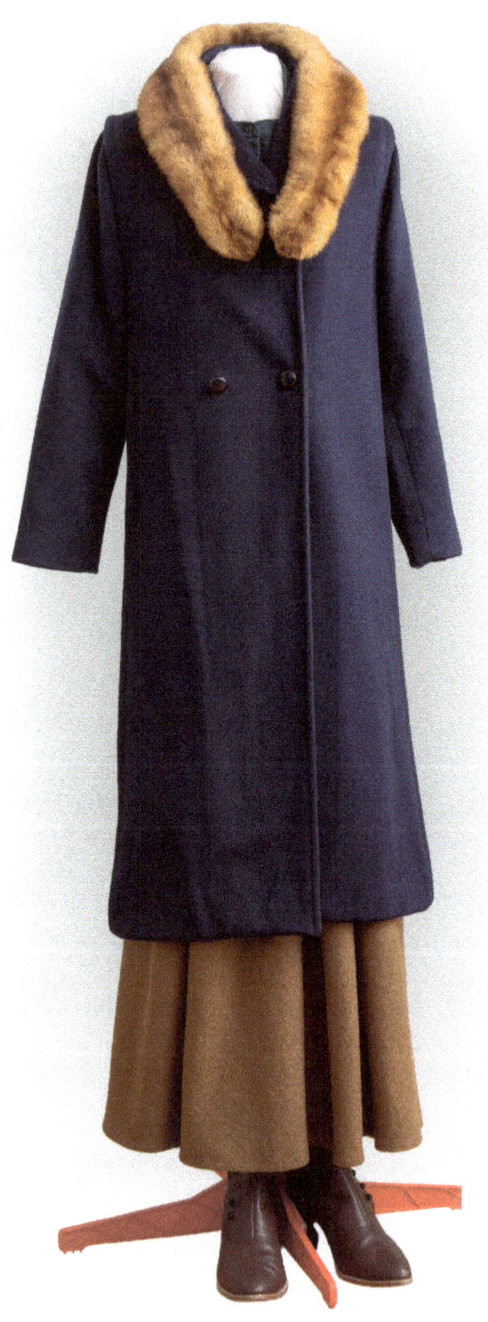

Figure 10. Better color harmony: knowledge of color theory will help to improve the beauty of an ensemble. (PHOTO BY CAMERON MCCARTY)

PROPORTION

Many Thomists will view proportion and harmony as overlapping if not synonymous principles. The Goldsteins themselves write that proportion is "the Law of Relationships," a definition hardly distinguishable from their words on harmony. But as one reads on, one soon sees that what the sisters mean by proportion is a more specialized treatment of shape harmony.[13]

The Goldsteins' treatment of proportion stems from an understanding of the human mind's tendency to assess rapidly (and subsequently dismiss) monotonous patterns such as the spacing on a picket fence, but to linger on unusual patterns such as a gate or archway. Their example *par excellence* from which they build their entire pedagogy of proportion is the Greek Parthenon, with its proportions of roughly two-to-three.

One-to-one ratios, such as those seen in the drop-waist frocks of the flappers, are dismissed by the Goldsteins as "mechanical," "uninteresting," and "commonplace."[14] The sisters provide detailed analysis of human proportions as measured by head-lengths, and they point out that women ought to remember that fashion figures are often drawn as nine, ten, or eleven heads tall, when the average woman is only seven-and-a-half heads tall. The sisters remind their students that harmonious proportions in dress must always begin with an understanding of the proportions and size of each individual. For instance, a broad woman ought to avoid wide horizontal stripes, as they will tend to make her appear overly broad and distract from her other features. A very petite woman ought to avoid oversized prints. For instance, flowers should never be bigger than the wearer's own head.

To further understand the principle of proportion, consider the following figures:

[13] Goldstein, 57.   [14] Goldstein, 59–66.

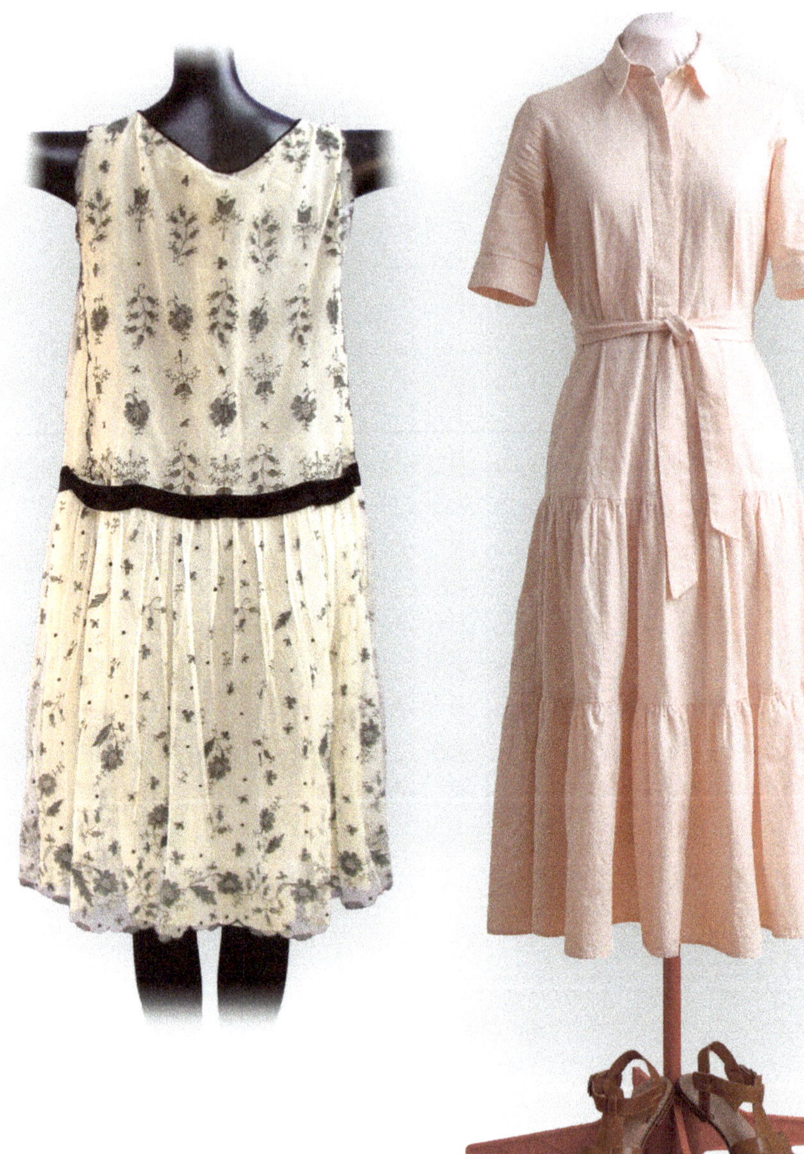

Figure 11. Ugly proportion: the Goldsteins particularly warned against waist lines that divided the figure in half. (SOURCE: AUCKLAND WAR MEMORIAL MUSEUM TĀMAKI PAENGA HIRA)

Figure 12. Beautiful proportion: the waist line here divides the dress into a roughly 2:3 ratio pleasing to the eye. (PHOTO: CAMERON MCCARTY)

Although the Goldsteins refer often to the "normal" and "average" figures with regard to height and provide much practical guidance for dressing the "stout" figure, they never mention dress of the pregnant woman.[15] This omission can likely be attributed to the times in which they wrote. However, given their focus on health and ease of motion, one can well imagine that the Goldsteins took the pregnant figure in stride. To the woman of "large waist and hips," they recommend building out the shoulders, keeping the center of interest at the face, wearing skirts long to add height, and selecting hats of slightly larger than average size.[16]

The model in Figure 13 is thirty-eight weeks pregnant. The structure and detailed stitching of her velvet jacket lend width to her shoulders, and her fur hat echoes the black of her dress while drawing the eye to her face. The use of these elements does not attempt to hide pregnancy, but, rather, creates an effect that protects the mother's sense of modesty and helps the viewer see the mother as a whole person. Where her pregnancy draws much attention to her body, simple techniques of dress can help draw the eye back to her face, the window of her soul.

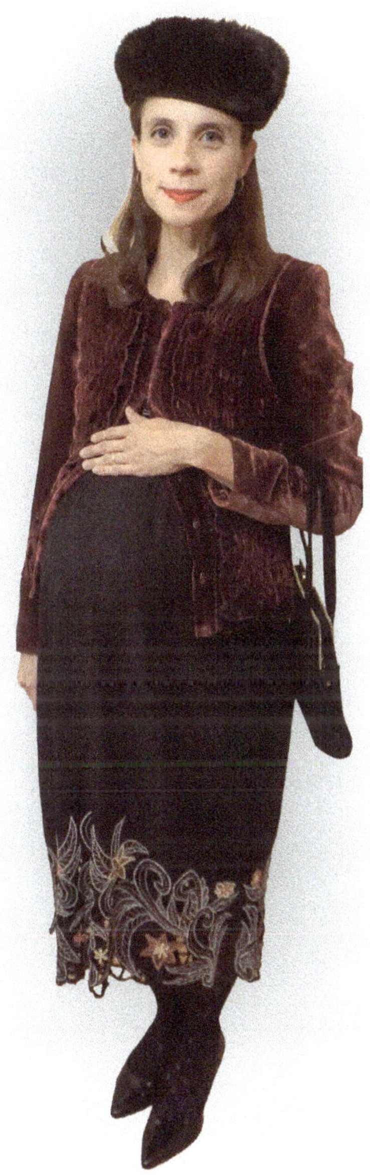

Figure 13. Successful harmony and proportion for the pregnant woman.
(PHOTO: ERIN WERNER)

[15] Goldstein, 302.   [16] Goldstein, 279.

BALANCE

The Goldsteins define balance as a restful effect obtained by grouping shapes and colors around a center in a way that creates equality of attractions on each side of that center. They illustrate the principle with a humorous example: "One does not enjoy watching a woman in the street if she is wearing a wide hat and large furs, with a short tight skirt and French heels; she looks so top-heavy that it seems as if the next gust of wind would blow her over."[17]

They then launch into a practical overview of how weights (sizes and colors) must balance a work of art across right and left and top and bottom. The Goldsteins use Pinturicchio's *Music* as an example of "formal balance," which occurs in symmetrical compositions:

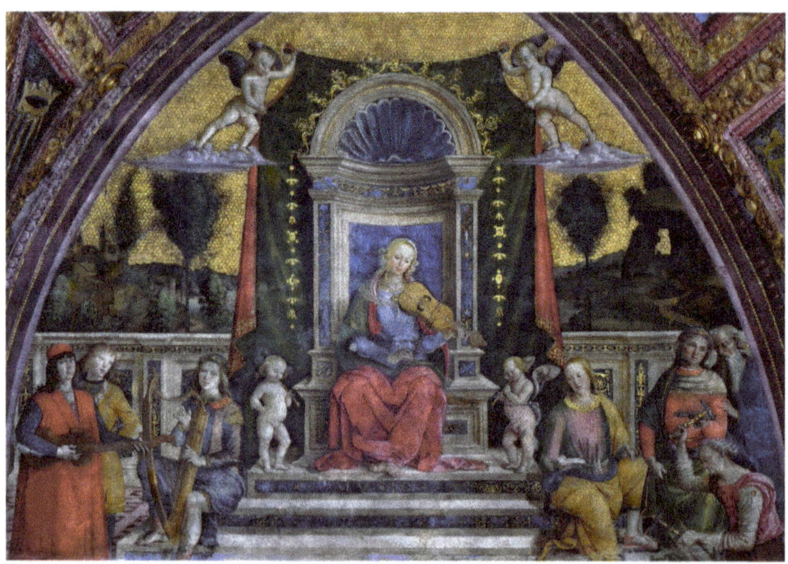

Figure 14. Formal balance: Pinturicchio's "Music" shows
objects arranged symmetrically to produce formal balance.

And they use Puvis de Chavannes's *Saint Geneviève Watching over Paris* to illustrate "informal balance," where the composition is not symmetrical but balanced by skillful spacing of objects and the use of varied depths of color.

[17] Goldstein, 83.

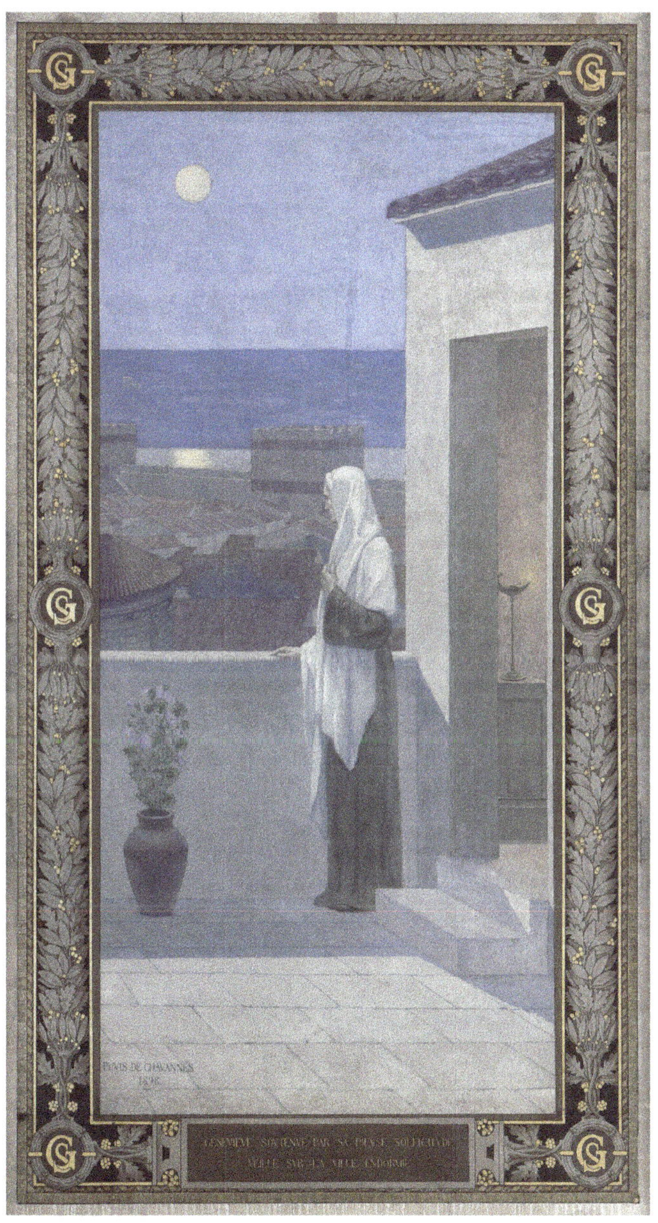

Figure 15. Informal balance: Pierre Puvis de Chavannes's "Saint Geneviève Watching over Paris" shows objects arranged asymmetrically but strategically with relation to the center to maintain balance.

One can achieve formal balance in dress more easily than informal balance because the human figure lends itself so well to symmetry: the figure has two arms, so two sleeves make good sense; the figure has width at the bust and at the hips, so flares in the fabric at both places balance each other perfectly.

A lady may achieve informal balance with such tricks as a corsage on her right shoulder and a large bracelet on her left hand, or by a scarf hung over her right side and a hat tilted to the left. However, attempts at more prominent asymmetry usually end in failure.

Modern designers often discard symmetry without any attempt at achieving beauty through informal balance. They make one-shoulder dresses or jagged skirt hems that hang ridiculously longer on one side without any element on the other to restore balance. One recent example is the wedding gown of Rajwa Alseif by Eli Saab, which featured diagonal gathers across the bodice and a neckline that veered sharply toward her right shoulder. This strong diagonal motion and the jarring shape created by the neckline were not counterbalanced by any other interesting line or shape in the ensemble.

The most common violation of balance seen among devout Catholics is the use of heavy shoes paired with skirts that hit right at mid-calf, making the figure bottom-heavy. While this appearance of bulkiness or cloddishness is of course unintentional among those of faith, it is celebrated by the destructive forces of popular culture, which drive mainstream fashion into ever greater ugliness.

Contrast Figure 16 with the ensemble in Figure 17 that shows perfect balance and feminine grace:

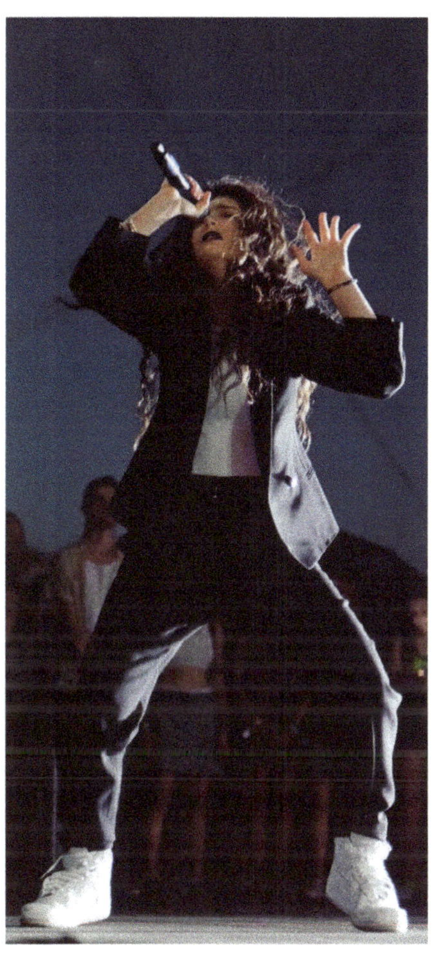

Figure 16. Unsuccessful balance:
bottom-heaviness caused by bulky
shoes of contrasting color. Nor is
that the only problem here. . .
(PHOTO: NEON TOMMY)

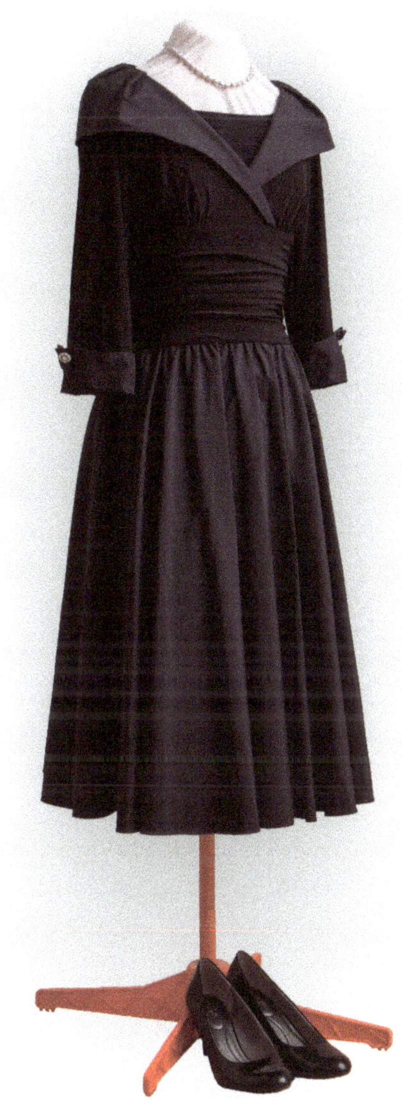

Figure 17. Successful balance.
(PHOTO: CAMERON MCCARTY)

RHYTHM

The Goldstein sisters define rhythm as the "easy, connected path along which the eye may travel in any arrangement of lines, colors, objects, or lights and darks."[18] In order to possess true rhythm, a work of art must allow the eyes this "ease" of movement, which provides a sense of rest. Aquinas tells us that happiness is "rest in a good attained."[19] The good attained from rhythm is the same as the good attained from any of the art principles, namely, the beauty of form. In other words, rhythm takes its part in bringing to bear the form (or the truth) through movement. Meaningless lines, chaotic patterns, and inharmonious combinations of textures and colors lack rhythm.

To further understand the principle of rhythm, consider the figures opposite.

Figure 18 shows an ensemble lacking rhythm. The eye does not rest, but, rather, throbs in the repetition of thin stripes over a large area, and the arrangement of these stripes, in a large zigzag, does not bring to bear a beautiful form, but seems at odds with the wearer's form, as if she had been slashed to pieces and reassembled incorrectly. The clashing yellow T-shirt creating yet another meaningless line at the hips only adds to the overall effect of chaos, and the straps of the sandals bring in another unrelated scheme.

Figure 19, on the other hand, shows lines that form an orderly pattern over the wearer's legs. The use of horizontal lines adds interest, but the predominant motion is vertical, which highlights the upright posture of the human form. The color palette is more complex than that in Figure 18, and yet the eye moves from one color to the next easily, as one word moves to another in a well-metered poem.

EMPHASIS

The Goldsteins define emphasis as "the art principle by which the eye is carried *first to the most important thing* in any arrangement, and from that point to every other detail *in the order of importance*."[20] The sisters highlight the importance of simplicity in a design—of having a clear center of interest that may or may not have secondary points of interest around it. "The eye and the mind do not enjoy

[18] Goldstein, 115.   [19] *Summa theologiae*, I-II, Q. 4, art. 1.   [20] Goldstein, 141.

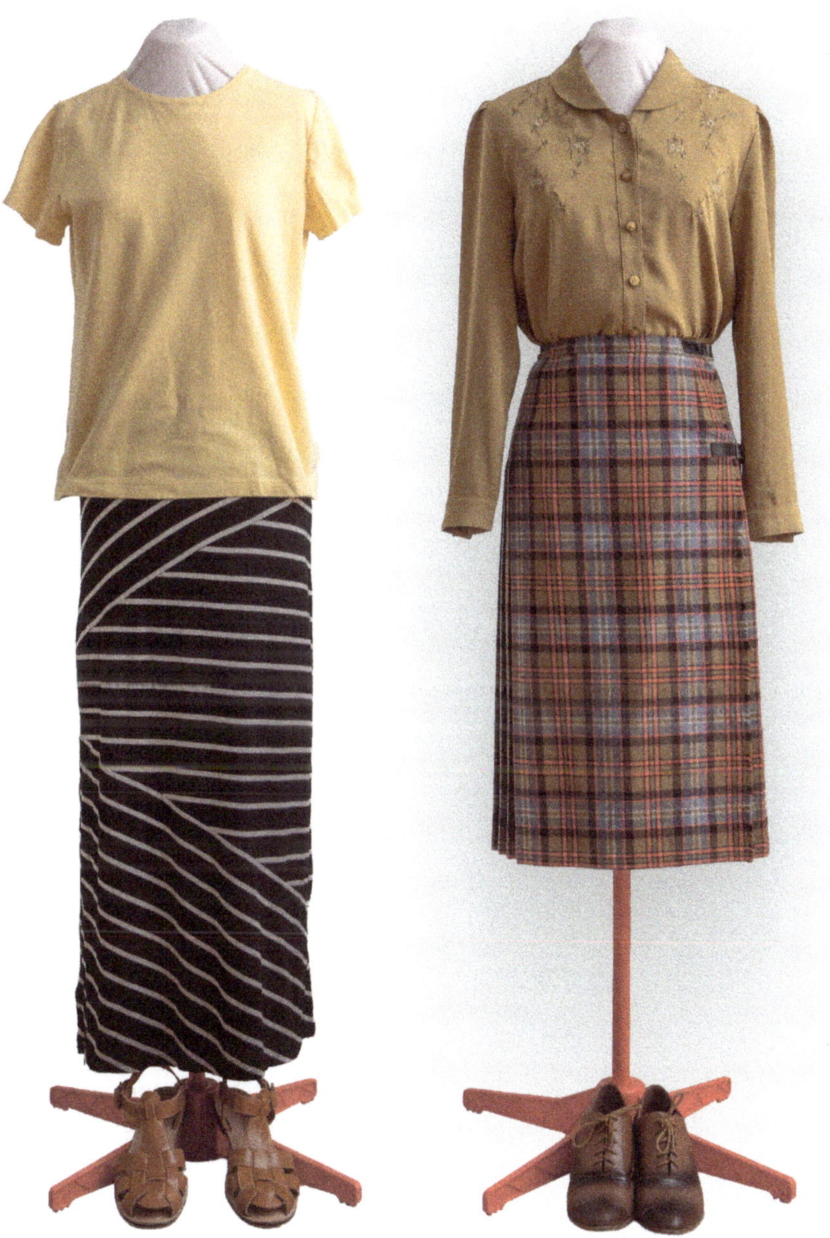

Figure 18. Lack of rhythm.
(PHOTO: CAMERON MCCARTY)

Figure 19. Successful rhythm.
(PHOTO: CAMERON MCCARTY)

a haphazard collection of shapes and colors," they state.[21] And lest their students mistake this tenet as a call to empty monotony, the Goldsteins present Hubert and Jan van Eyck's *Adoration of the Lamb* as a composition far from minimalistic, but possessing an unmistakable center and several secondary points of interest:

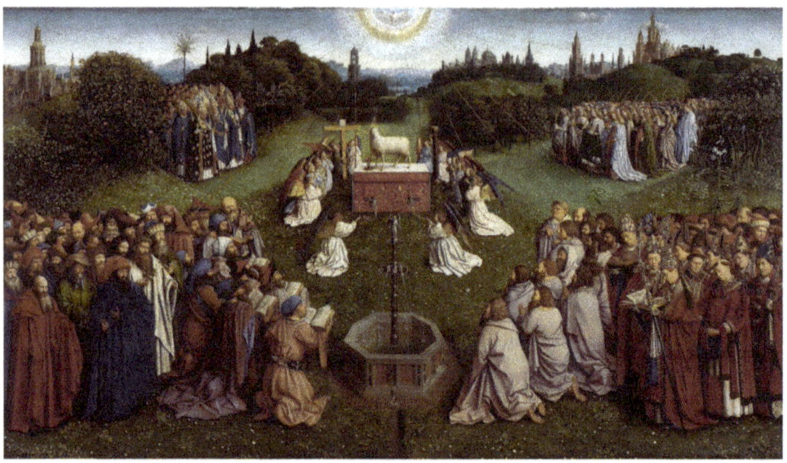

Figure 20. Successful emphasis.

To help their students bring about successful emphasis in their own compositions, the Goldsteins exhort them to carefully consider the following questions:

- What to emphasize?
- How to emphasize?
- How much to emphasize?
- Where to place emphasis?[22]

They then discuss each of these questions at length and provide insights on grouping of elements, contrasting lights and darks, ornamentation, judging the correct ratio of background space, and the use of unusual or unexpected lines, shapes, sizes, and colors. Emphasis, in comparison to the other art principles, demands subtle artistic judgment. Where the other principles seem almost binary—e.g., one achieves harmony or disharmony, balance or imbalance, and

---

[21] Goldstein, 141.   [22] Ibid.

so on—emphasis exists on a more gradual scale and has the added pitfall that one may very successfully emphasize the wrong thing.

Modern clothing designers have become masters of the principle of emphasis, but they choose to emphasize what ought actually to be veiled. Deep V-necks, "window shirts," and "cold shoulder shirts" draw the eye to cleavage or reveal patches of flesh with the sole purpose of impelling the mind to lust for still more naked flesh. Great slits in the skirts of evening gowns point like arrows at the body beneath as if to apologize to the lusting viewer for such a troublesome excess of fabric. All but the baggiest of women's blue jeans are designed to draw the eyes to the wearer's buttocks.[23] Finally, yoga pants and clinging T-shirts adhere to every curve like the casing of a sausage, making the human within appear like only so much meat.

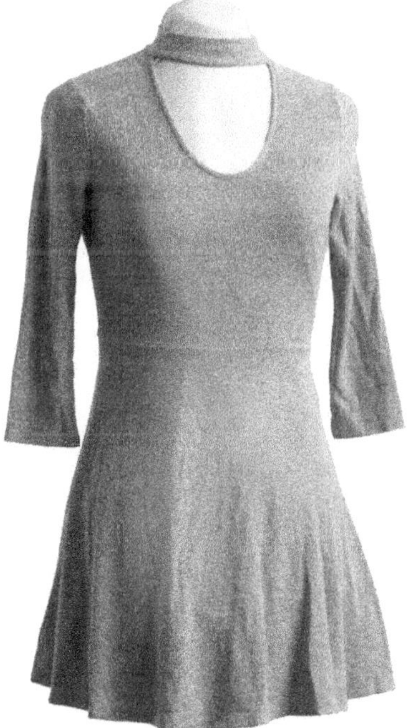

Figure 21. Undesirable emphasis: the "window shirt" draws eyes away from the face. (PHOTO: CAMERON MCCARTY)

[23] "Stylist Stacy London Says Skinny Jeans Will Never Die—Here's Why," *Rachel Ray Show,* 2021. In this video tutorial on denim selection, stylist Stacy London tells viewers, "The most important thing to know about denim is that if it doesn't make your butt look good, you're wearing the wrong shape."

The Goldstein sisters take a different approach to emphasis. They write, "In the well-organized plan for a costume the face will be the chief center of interest; the most successful design is that which will lead the eye to the face through the choice and arrangement of all the colors and lines that go to make up a dress design."[24] And elsewhere: "Here the person is the chief center of interest, and the clothes are the background."[25] Emphasis of the face, however, does not mean that clothing must be bland or have no points of interest of its own. The sisters explain how Bronzino's *Portrait of Lucrezia Panciatichi* (Figure 22) centers the viewer's interest on her face by way of an ornate neckline echoed at her waist with a jeweled belt. The eyes then fall to her beautiful hands, which are emphasized both by the contrast of dark fabric with light flesh and by the delicate ruffles of her cuffs. Her exposed neck and hands do not distract from her face but, rather, complement it, and she sits before the viewer as a truly whole person.[26]

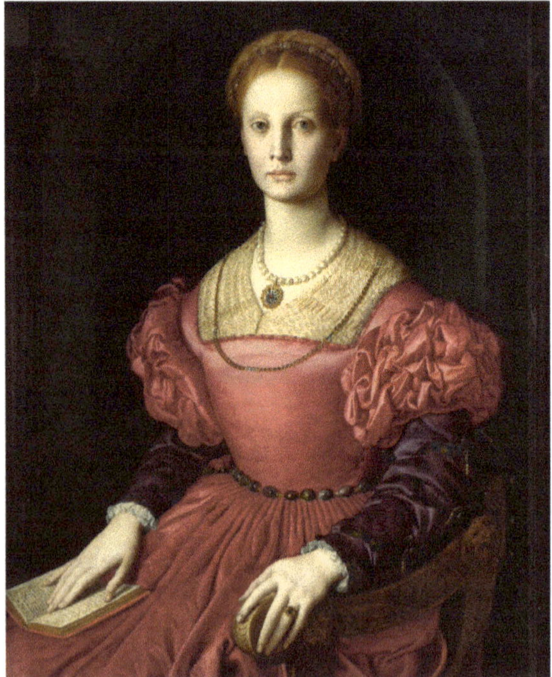

Figure 22. Emphasis that is successful from
both moral and artistic standpoints.

[24] Goldstein, *Art in Everyday Life*, 167.   [25] Goldstein, 164.   [26] Goldstein, 169.

In dress, there exist many possible secondary points of interest, but, in general, any feature not overtly sexual may add to the beauty of the whole without leading to lust. For instance, a woman may show the beauty of her collar bones with a neckline cut just a little beneath them; this emphasis, rather than drawing the eye down in the way of a deep V-neck, draws the eye back up to the face by framing it. Or a woman may wear an ornamented belt that divides her figure in pleasing proportion without revealing every curve.

Figure 23 shows a contemporary example of an ensemble where the neckline (highlighted by pearls) and the waist (highlighted by a sash) add interest, but exist only as parts of the whole and will emphasize rather than distract from the wearer's face.

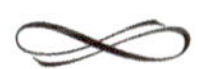

Writing in the wake of World War I, the Goldsteins would have noticed early signs of cultural decay all around them, yet their book betrays no alarm. For better or for worse, they did not fill their pages with laments and admonishments, only with calm, commonplace instruction. Nor did they consider the application of art principles an

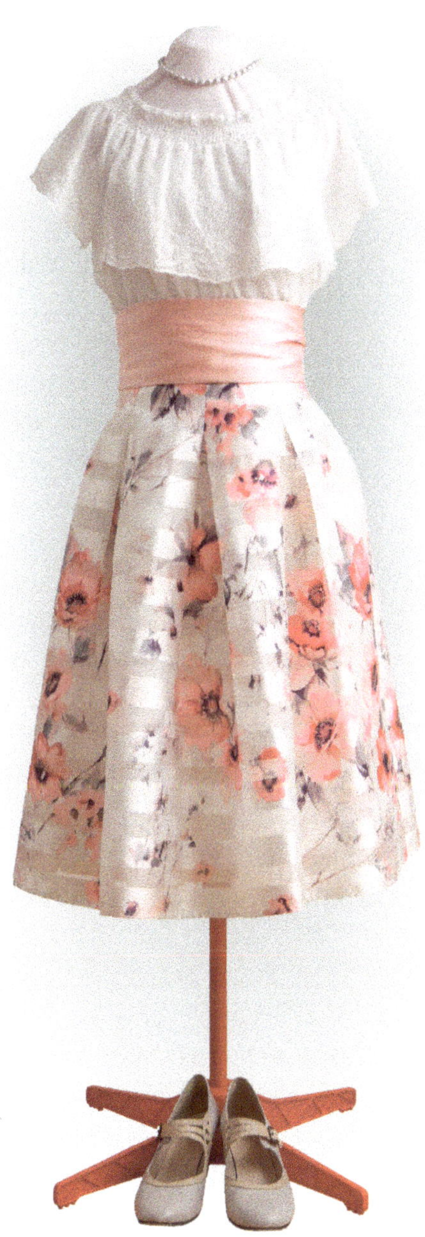

Figure 23. Morally and artistically successful emphasis.
(PHOTO: CAMERON MCCARTY)

act of "restoration"; it was merely an act of good taste. Though they admitted that dressing well requires study and care, they never went so far as to say that it requires courage and perseverance.

But for us today, the art principles call for a more concerted and whole-hearted adoption. Whereas, in the Goldsteins' day, art principles acted as guidelines to help consumers make selections in the market's plethora of readily available options, they now act as beacons in a cultural wasteland where options are few and far between.

Nevertheless, causes for hope abound. For one thing, the principles themselves are as simple as ever; merely by thinking about them as she selects her daily clothing, a woman will begin to discover how she might improve her dress. She need not transform her entire wardrobe overnight; it is enough to begin with just one ensemble. For another thing, the increase of small online boutiques and resources for seamstresses has allowed women to break free from the tyranny of the shopping mall's and superstore's inferior offerings. Finally, readers will find that the beauty they achieve as they apply the art principles becomes a real source of nourishment to themselves and those around them. This nourishment will help them continue on with the quest to still more beauty. By practicing dress as a joyful art rather than a dreary duty, women give the world a view of higher things, of the life of the soul, and even of heaven itself.

FIVE WAYS TO BEGIN APPLYING THE ART PRINCIPLES NOW

1. Begin with Solemn Mass. Consider the clothing you usually wear to Solemn Mass and start by perfecting just one ensemble. Do the elements harmonize with the shape of your body? Your age? Your personality? The color of your skin and hair? Do the elements bear a family relationship with each other? Are there elements of denim or rustic leather that could be replaced with something more suitable for a solemn liturgy? (One question that can often help: would I wear this to a wedding? If not, then it is not suitable for Sunday Mass.) Do the ensemble's rhythms provide rest to the eyes? Would a hat or graceful shawl improve the ensemble's balance?

Does the ensemble emphasize that which should be veiled? Or, if the emphasis is properly on the face, would a belt, sash, or necklace add an interesting secondary point of emphasis?

2. Enjoy dress every day. Even if one dresses for messy housework or errands, one can still enjoy practicing the art principles. An old, baggy dress from a thrift store can receive new shape with the use of a belt. A festive cotton scarf that harmonizes with skirt and blouse can hold back hair. Aprons of all shapes and sizes can take much of the risk out of working in "nicer" clothing. Few tasks besides mucking stalls and painting rooms are so messy that even a full-body apron will not suffice to protect one's ensemble.

3. Look for quality over quantity. Rather than filling your closet with scores of polyester dresses of a generic one-size-fits-most design, save your funds to buy one dress or skirt of cotton, linen, or wool from an online vendor that provides customization options to suit your size, shape, and personal taste.

4. Be patient. It took you time (probably years) to build your current wardrobe. Do not try to overturn it in one day. Work with what you have as best you can and be selective with new purchases.

5. Remember for Whom you dress. The whole point of dressing beautifully is to draw your mind and heart to God. If ever the difficulty of practicing the art of dress begins to discourage you, remember to offer your efforts to Christ Who clothes the lilies of the field.

4

Elegance versus Beauty

O N READING THE PREVIOUS chapter, a reader might observe that, although I promote beautiful dress in the abstract, the illustrations I present fall short of beauty; they are, rather, what we might more aptly describe as just pretty or elegant.

The truth of the matter is that contemporary dress lacks beauty. By contemporary dress, I mean not only shapeless T-shirts, yoga pants, and ripped jeans, but also the very best that today's society can muster. Certainly, we may still find clothing that we call pretty or elegant, but, for an ensemble to deserve the epithet of beautiful, it must possess some mark of excellence far above our typical Sunday best, and it is this excellence that virtually all modern clothing lacks.[1]

In his *Aesthetics*, Dietrich von Hildebrand presents the "family" of aesthetic values that includes, among others, the lovely, the pretty, the charming, the graceful, the poetic, and the sublime. The queen of the aesthetic values is beauty.[2] Hildebrand goes on to make an important distinction between beauty and elegance. The latter value he identifies as "this-worldly," whereas beauty is "other-worldly." Though he considers elegance certainly within the family of aesthetic values and closely related to gracefulness, he sees it also as rooted in the mundane. Elegance, Hildebrand writes, "has no place in eternity."[3] This careful delineation of aesthetical terms helps to explain the tension one feels when pondering paintings that depict

---

[1] Hildebrand, *Aesthetics*, 1:81.   [2] Hildebrand, 1:77.   [3] Hildebrand, 1:399–400.

certain modern saints clad in three-piece suits or physicians' jackets among the choirs of heaven. While saints of former centuries have enjoyed truly beautiful raiment that transposes easily to portrayals of the heavenly court, the clothing of modern saints, elegant at best, invariably strikes a discordant note. Even the best artist cannot properly apotheosize a man wearing trousers and a necktie.

To further explore the difference between elegance and beauty, let us consider the figures below:

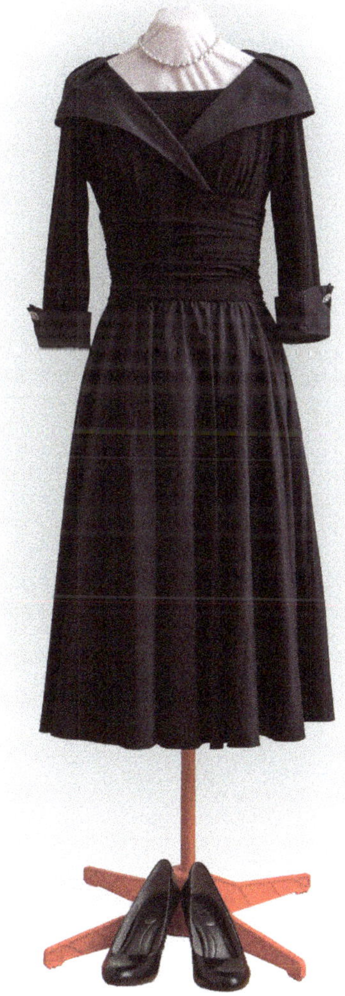

Figure 1. An elegant dress.
(PHOTO: CAMERON MCCARTY)

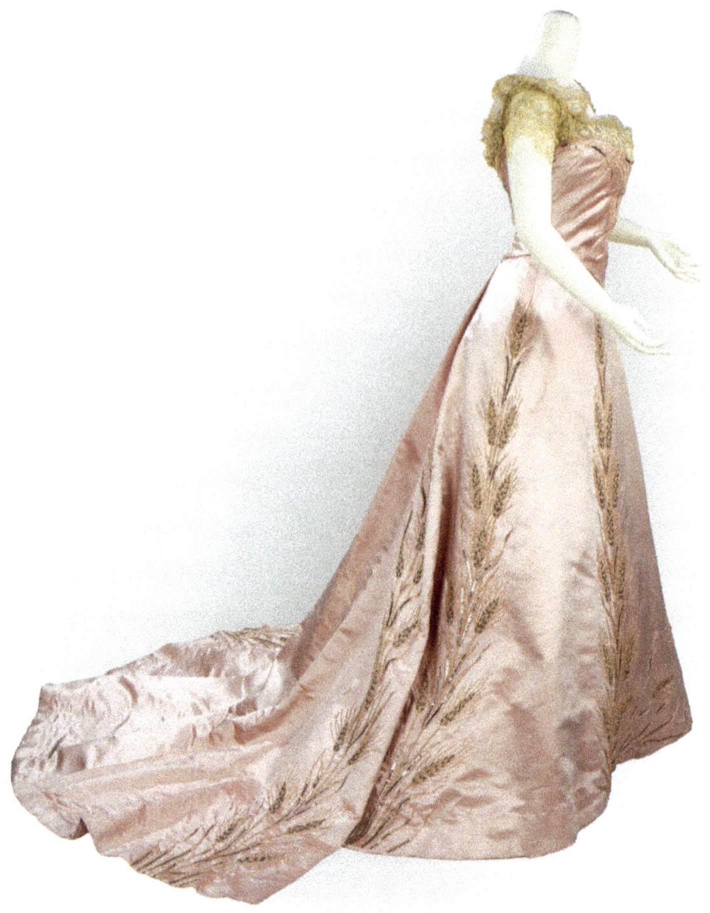

Figure 2. A beautiful dress. (SOURCE: THE METROPOLITAN MUSEUM OF ART)

In Figure 1, we see a contemporary evening dress inspired by the New Look of the 1950s. I use this dress often to demonstrate the successful application of the principles of harmony, proportion, balance, rhythm, and emphasis. Its quiet grace, clean lines, and indisputable air of refinement make it an apt illustration of elegance. The dress in Figure 2, designed in 1900 by the House of Worth, also possesses grace, but now it is a sweeping, radiant grace, at once more youthful and more regal than that of the black dress. The curved lines suggesting the petals of a lily, the abundance of precious fabric, and the exquisite ornamentation of embroidery and gold needle lace all do their part to make the gown truly beautiful.

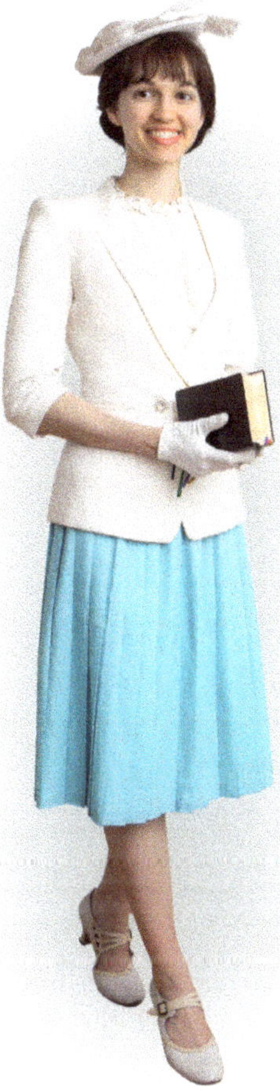

Figure 3. A moderately
elegant suit. Contemporary.
(PHOTO: CAMERON MCCARTY)

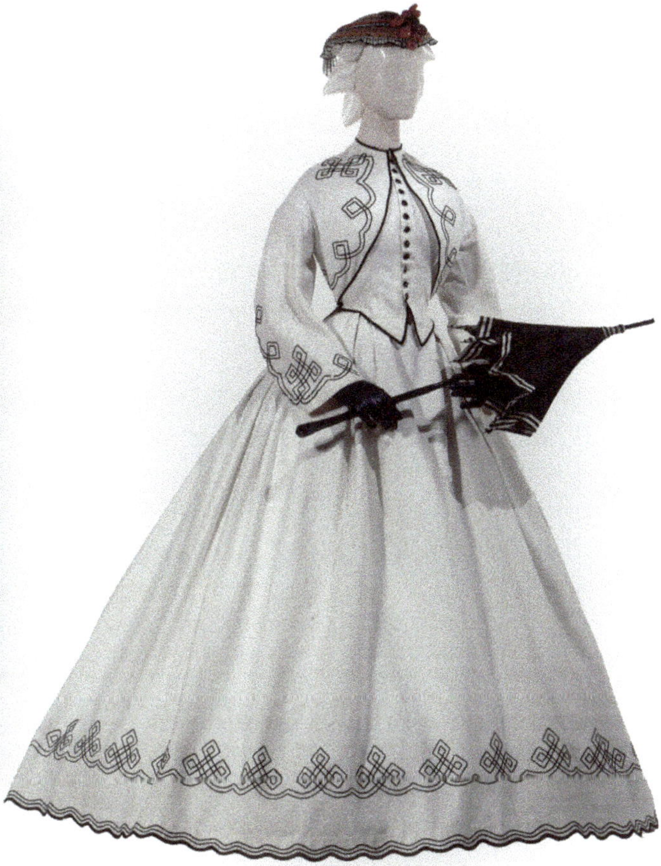

Figure 4. A very elegant promenade
dress. 1860s. (SOURCE: THE
METROPOLITAN MUSEUM OF ART)

It is interesting to note that within the realm of the elegant itself, one finds a spectrum on which some items bear more grace and draw nearer to that other-worldly quality of beauty than others. Above are two examples that illustrate different degrees of elegance.

In Figure 3, we see a contemporary Easter Sunday suit inspired by the style of the 1940s. A pleated skirt and a jacket worn with chiffon ruffles at the throat, a feathered hat, gloves, and feminine shoes combine to make a relatively elegant lady's ensemble. But compare this to a promenade dress of the 1860s, which perhaps was once also worn on an

Easter Sunday (Figure 4). Immediately, one notices that the promenade dress exudes a certain fullness and grace that the modern suit lacks. Contrast the two skirts: the suit's short skirt forms a stiff rectangle over the legs; the promenade dress's splendid bell does not cut across the legs, but flows gracefully in one continuous curve over them. Next note the suit jacket, all angles and stark lines, the style Christian Dior disparaged as that worn by "soldier-women with shoulders like boxers."[4] Compare these sharp lines to those that make up the promenade dress's Zouave-style jacket. From the wrists to the earlobes, the Zouave jacket draws two S-curves along its sleeves like the graceful scrolled arms on either side of a Grecian vase. Note again the S-curves flowing down from the jacket's closure at the throat, across the bosom, and along the bell of the skirt. At the hem of the skirt, one finds yet another homage to the S-curve in charming embroidery playfully echoed and expanded upon throughout the ensemble. And how can one not but marvel at the perfect craftsmanship of the fitted bodice, so trim, and yet not in the least departing from the beauty of the feminine form?

While the lines of the contemporary suit do have their aesthetic appeal, cutting what one might call a "smart" figure, the promenade dress's fullness, generated by a graceful symphony of curves, tells more truly of feminine nature and speaks of something higher and more noble than the merely sophisticated woman.

And yet, notwithstanding the undeniable artistic success of the promenade dress in Figure 4, it does, in the end, possess elegance rather than beauty. Like much of Victorian fashion, the dress bears an ineluctable spirit of modernity that firmly ties it to this world. The Victorians' romanticism still fostered ideals like the graceful feminine curves aided by voluminous skirts, but the creeping spirits of hurry and egalitarianism, fueled by growing industrialization, left their mark. Women found they could have those voluminous skirts without the weight of petticoats or the expense of the hand-crafted wooden panniers of the previous century; they only needed steel cage-crinolines, fruits of some of the world's first mass-production.[5]

---

4 Przybyszewski, *Lost Art of Dress*, 30.
5 "Cage Crinoline," *Fashion History Timeline*, https://fashionhistory.fitnyc.edu/cage-crinoline/.

Women no longer needed linen from the village weaver; those yards of cotton pique came from global trade and great industrial mills.[6] In short, Victorian dress presents an ironic juxtaposition of the highest ideals and all that led to their demise.

Shifting the discussion again to the beautiful, consider the excellent example of beautiful dress found in Goya's painting *The Parasol* in Figure 5.

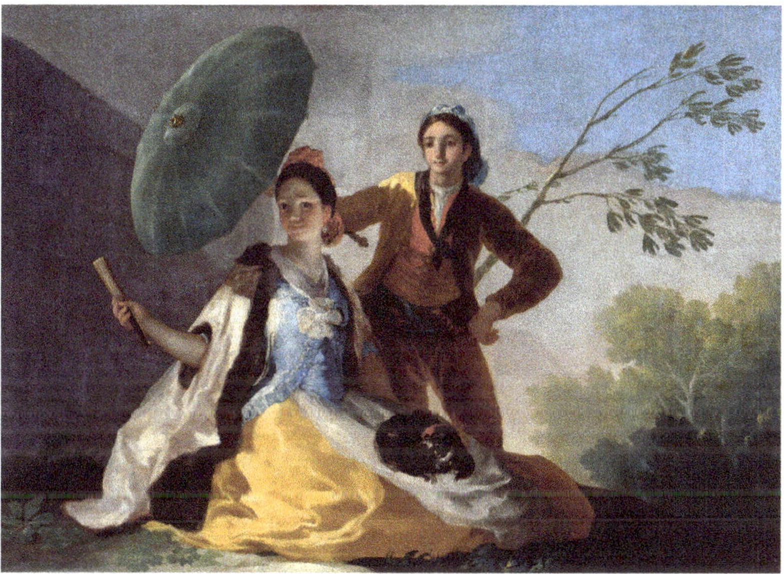

Figure 5. Example of beautiful dress. (SOURCE: MUSEO DEL PRADO)

While the clothes of this lady and her servant conform to the fashions of their day (the 1770s),[7] they also possess a timeless quality. Fruits of art and the prevailing culture, and not mere products of industrialization, their clothing transcends the zeitgeist and speaks of something high and profound.

Figure 6 shows another example of a beautiful dress. In it, one finds the tell-tale characteristics of grace, length of line, fullness, and timelessness.

[6] "The Fall of the Weavers," *Monkey Town: The History of Heywood*, https://www.heywoodhistory.com/2016/06/fall-of-weavers.html.
[7] "The Parasol 1777," *Costume Cocktail*, https://www.costumecocktail.com/2016/12/04/the-parasol-1777/.

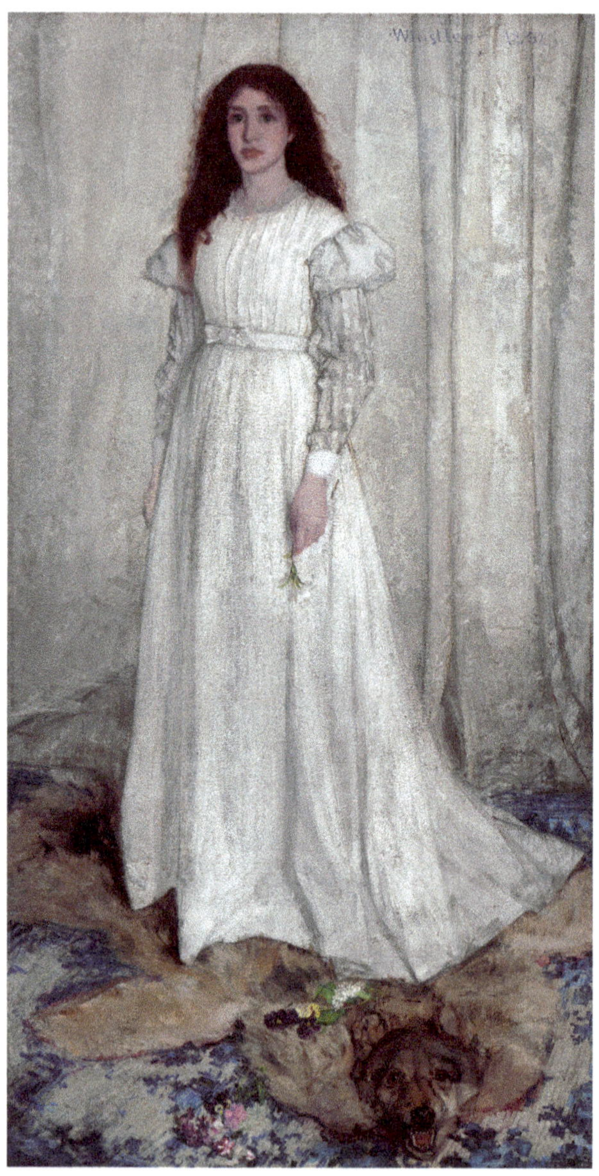

Figure 6. An example of the timelessness of beauty.
James McNeill Whistler, "Symphony in White, No. 1: The White Girl."

Next, compare Figure 7 with my description of a contemporary gown worn recently by the (then) Duchess of Cambridge.

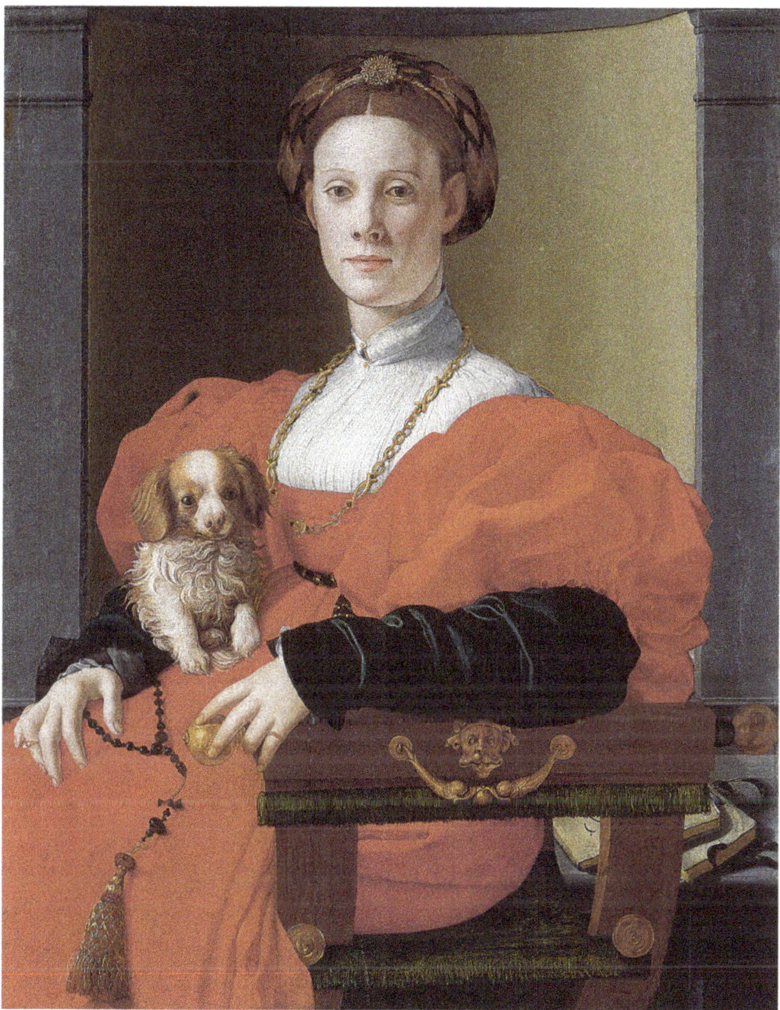

Figure 7. Beautiful dress. Agnolo Bronzino, "Portrait of a Lady in Red."
(SOURCE: STÄDEL MUSEUM, FRANKFURT AM MAIN)

In Figure 7, we see a gown of stunning beauty. Its shape, its volume, its color, all contribute to its message of unearthly grandeur, while not diminishing its warmth and femininity. There is here, as in my other examples of beauty, a theme of abundance, even superfluity. Why should the lady's puffed sleeves be so full? Why should she have silk velvet undersleeves? Why lace cuffs beneath those? Why a skirt so voluminous that it pushes against the arm of the chair? Why must she have rings, a headband, a belt, *and* a chain? Is she not the quintessence of what post-moderns love to dismiss as "a bit much"? She is certainly a bit much if one holds her up to the prosaic and utilitarian standard of the present day. "With sleeves that wide, she'd have trouble fitting through doors!" a philistine will jeer. Or, "I'd be smothered by that much fabric!" a young girl, taught from her earliest years to view all historical dress as oppressive, might say. And yet, in looking at the lady, one finds no frivolity; there is nothing one wishes to strip away from her, nothing that mars or distracts. One wishes, rather, to rise to her standard.

Now contrast the above ensemble, regal and yet gentle, with my description of the Roland Mouret gown worn by the (then) Duchess of Cambridge at the 2022 *Top Gun: Maverick* premier. (Photos of this gown are easily found online.) A form-fitting column of black intersected by a hard band of white that seems to bind the shoulders, the gown imposes itself, almost brutally, on the Duchess. Her tight, muscular form emerges from the garment as if she'd had a power struggle with it—and barely won. The stark contrast of black and white adds to the sense of tension the dress generates. A fitting design, perhaps, for a celebration of fighter jets, the Mouret gown does nothing to reveal woman's true beauty. It lacks grace, poetry, and any reference to eternity. Made for red carpets and flashbulbs, gowns like this may have a certain aesthetic appeal, but that appeal is, at best, merely elegance. Needless to say, such appeals often stray into the realm of immodesty, appearing low and cheap and stirring man's animal passions.

For another comparison between elegance and beauty, consider a fashion plate from the 1930s (Figure 8) and costumes of the Italian Renaissance (Figure 9). Of course, the dresses of the fashion plate achieve artistic success, and, relative to anything available on the market today, they are excellent. Nevertheless, they pale in comparison to the gowns of the Italian Renaissance.

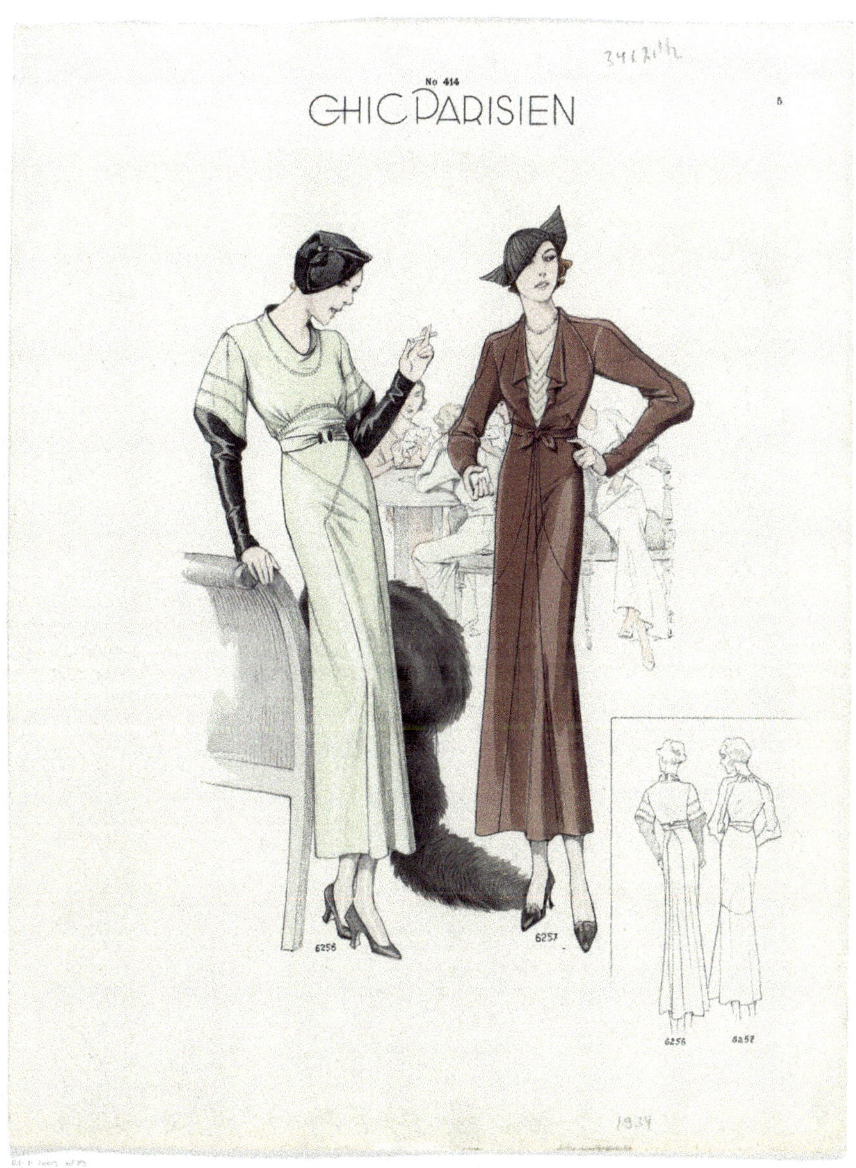

Figure 8. Elegance. (SOURCE: *Chic Parisien*, NO. 414)

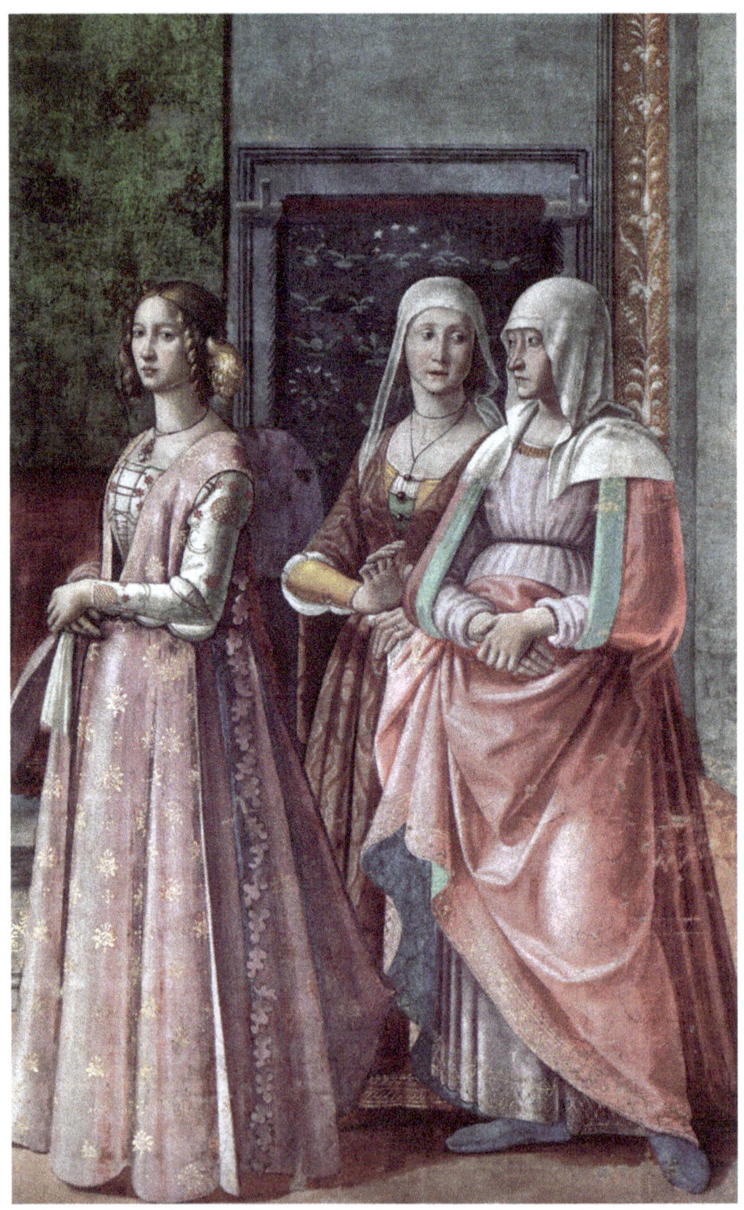

Figure 9. Beauty. Cappella Tornabuoni, Florence:
"Birth of Saint John the Baptist" (detail).

Next, consider Filippo Lippi's *Madonna and Child* (Figure 10):

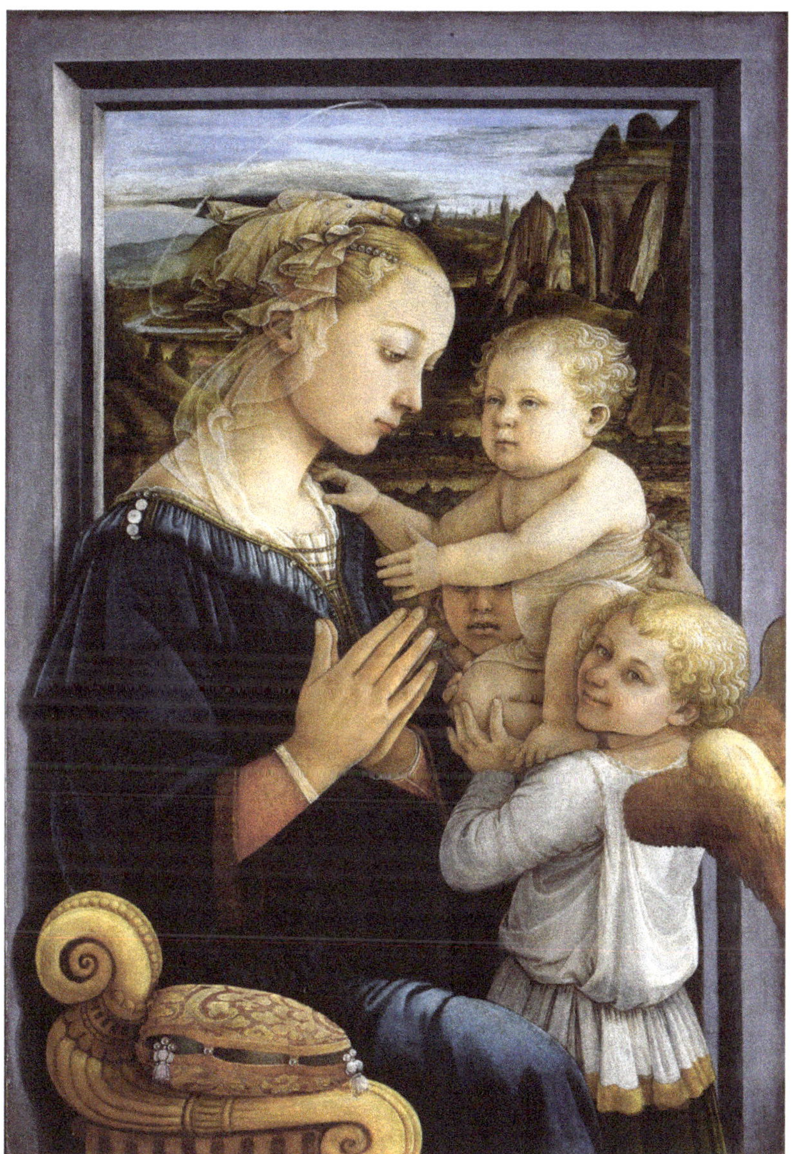

Figure 10. Beauty worthy of heaven.

Although Our Lady is portrayed here in the fashionable dress of the Italian Renaissance, there exists no discord between the spiritual theme of the painting and her clothing. The beauty of the clothing, rather than drawing the mind to the banal, lifts the mind to heaven, thus giving wings to the painting's theme. But if one were to see a painting depicting Our Lady in the clothing of the 1930s fashion plate, one would instinctively recoil. The elegance of fashion, which we may admire and choose for ourselves, we immediately perceive as far inferior to the beauty always owed to Our Lady.

But if beauty is superior to mere elegance, why, then, when I present the art principles, do I illustrate them with examples that are only elegant? The answer to this question is simply that I choose to promote fashion that stands some chance of resumption in our present day. This pedagogical choice is not at all because I see the elegant as the apex of cultural restoration; actually, elegance is only a stop-gap measure, a concession which allows us some relief from ugliness while we wait for better days. The alarming truth is that culture, in the words of Hildebrand, has been "strangled by civilization."[8] Culture has fallen into such a state of decay, and art has reached such a state of perversion, that the world no longer has a place for beautiful clothing. Our daily environments have lost the "poetry of life"[9] in which all the beauty of practical life (and clothes are a primary part of this) can be at home. In the following statement, Hildebrand identifies the root of the problem:

> The depoeticizing of the space we inhabit, which is profoundly linked to industrialization, goes hand in hand with a lack of interest in adequate external expression, and with a loss of the meaning and value of the 'forming' of our life. This is the victory of comfort and usefulness over beauty.[10]

Certainly, a clever seamstress might choose her preferred historical period and make for herself any number of beautiful articles according to the fashions therein. But in wearing these long-lost fashions, she would find that, because the world has cut itself off from beauty, she has, in a sense, cut herself off from the world. The "adequate external expression" that she wishes to convey to the world around her, i.e., beauty, meets its dull ears like the words of a foreign language; it cannot understand.

---

[8] Hildebrand, *Aesthetics*, 2:52.   [9] Hildebrand, 1:4.   [10] Hildebrand, 1:400.

Dress is, in fact, a language. Julian Kwasniewski expands upon this notion:

> Like language, and as a language of sorts, clothing is a mark of belonging in a communicative society. Clothing is an aspect of our being social animals; we are not, in fact, like the brute animals who do not create, discover, and communicate meaning through custom and culture.[11]

All throughout history, one sees a veritable lexicon of clothing customs: to name a few, the cloth of gold reserved for royalty,[12] the head-coverings of married women of any class, and the vast array of geographically-linked ornamentation in the world's folk traditions.

As soon as a man dresses, he conveys a message and asserts some meaning; he cannot fail to do so. If we argue that the ranks of our contemporaries who dress perpetually according to the athleisure imperative have no particular message to communicate, we are wrong; their clothing proclaims their message with perfect eloquence; namely, that all is *meaningless*. In a blur of digitally anesthetized despair, they drift through lives of bleak boredom captured in the popular song lyric: "Nothing's wrong when nothing's true. I live in a hologram with you."[13]

How can we respond? If even the proverbial "clever seamstress" cannot, by the sheer force of her skill, resuscitate beautiful dress, then what hope have we who find ourselves at the mercy of the mass market?

I once attended a lecture on the theory of entropy, that is, the world's tendency to devolve into ever greater disorder. The professor of physics showed a video of a wine glass falling to the floor and shattering. He stated, "This is entropy." Then he showed the video rewound. Shards of glass jumped off the floor and fused back together into the original flawless vessel. The professor flatly concluded, "This never happens." Likewise with dress: how easy to shatter; how difficult to restore.

[11] Julian Kwasniewski, "Do We Dress for Beauty?," *Tradition and Sanity*, December 7, 2023, https://traditionsanity.substack.com/p/do-we-dress-for-beauty.
[12] Daniel Roche, *The Culture of Clothing* (Cambridge University Press, 1996), 39–49.
[13] Lorde, "Buzzcut Season," track 6 on *Pure Heroine*. Republic Records, 2013.

Nevertheless, our throes of cultural decay notwithstanding, the fact that we will not, in our day, see a return to the fashions of the Italian Renaissance (or any other beautiful mode of dress) does not preclude the possibility, or rather the responsibility, to use whatever is left of the language of dress in its highest possible form. Our efforts may be pathetic, like the slurred and halting words of a stroke-survivor attempting his first rounds of speech therapy, but still we must press on. To do anything else is to concede to the anti-culture of despair.

A religious sister once encouraged me by saying, "It's not difficult to form a sub-culture. You just get a small group of people who don't care about being different, and you all start being different together." Communities of tradition-loving Catholics often provide fertile ground for the restoration of dress. A traditional parish almost always draws like-minded families to celebrate solemn festal occasions in which a latitude of expression in dress rarely seen elsewhere is not only possible, but the norm. Such communities function as incubators in which people may come and try new ideas (which are really old ideas) together. Suits, veils, hats, gloves, stockings, even capes, all obsolete in the mainstream, show up in abundance at a given traditional Mass. Of course, outside of Mass in the community's various social activities, still more opportunities for creativity abound.

Admittedly, the admonition to "just try your best" is a paltry solution to a dire problem, but the truth is, a return to a beautiful way of dress will take gigantic societal shifts that no person today has the power to enact. One such shift is a return to beautiful architecture. We will never feel completely at ease in beautiful clothing until the buildings we inhabit are once again beautiful. Another such shift is a restoration of hierarchical structures in society that allow for a differentiation between the various states and stations in the Christian life. Not everyone needs to dress in the silks of the nobility, but at least some should; and those who don't ought to have some other dignified attire clearly born of their environment, their work, and their local customs. At present, our globalized and egalitarian society has neither the beauty of an aristocracy, nor the charm of a folk tradition. C.S. Lewis puts it well:

> This is, indeed, part of the general problem of a classless
> society, which is too seldom mentioned. Will its *ethos* be
> a synthesis of what was best in all the classes, or a mere
> "pool" with the sediment of all and the virtues of none?[14]

Does not the state of dress today clearly demonstrate that we have, indeed, "the virtues of none"? And so, unable to transform abysmal architecture and failed social systems, we realize that we can only do small things and hope for better days. It does bear noting that, because standards have fallen to such lows, even a return to elegance will be a remarkable step forward for the cause of restoration. And yet, all the while that we strive for elegance, we must remember how inferior this earth-bound aesthetic value is to beauty, the queen of all aesthetic values. We must persistently fight complacency and false contentment.

Espousing this attitude of artistic discontent, we will surely draw accusations of snobbery and tone-deafness. How can one recommend fragile linen dresses priced at two or three hundred dollars, when Amazon has indestructible polyester frocks for twenty? For that matter, how dare one quibble about the fine points of dress at all when many a devout mother struggles to feed and educate her eight children? But such questions spring from faulty logic. Difficulty feeding the children is a problem. *And* ugly dress is a problem. We must accept that both problems exist rather than dismissing the importance of the latter as long as the former prevails.

All that writers like myself can do is present the problem clearly, describe how the problem was treated in the past, hazard one or two suggestions, and trust that the same spirit which guides us to write in the first place may also guide readers to take up their parts in the restoration with creativity, prudence, and holy zeal.

---

[14] C. S. Lewis, "The Necessity of Chivalry," in *Present Concerns*, ed. Walter Hopper (Harper Collins 1986), 6.

5
Materials

IN DECEMBER, 1888, ELLEN TERRY APPEARED as Lady Macbeth at London's Lyceum Theatre. She wore a gown adorned with beetle wings. Only nature could supply the wanted eerie shimmer in that era before plastic sequins.[1] Michael Jackson and countless others have since shimmered more than Ellen Terry ever did, but somehow, in these latter instances, after that initial dazzling flash, our enthusiasm fades. These modern shows of plastic are, after all, tame and tawdry. Terry's gown,

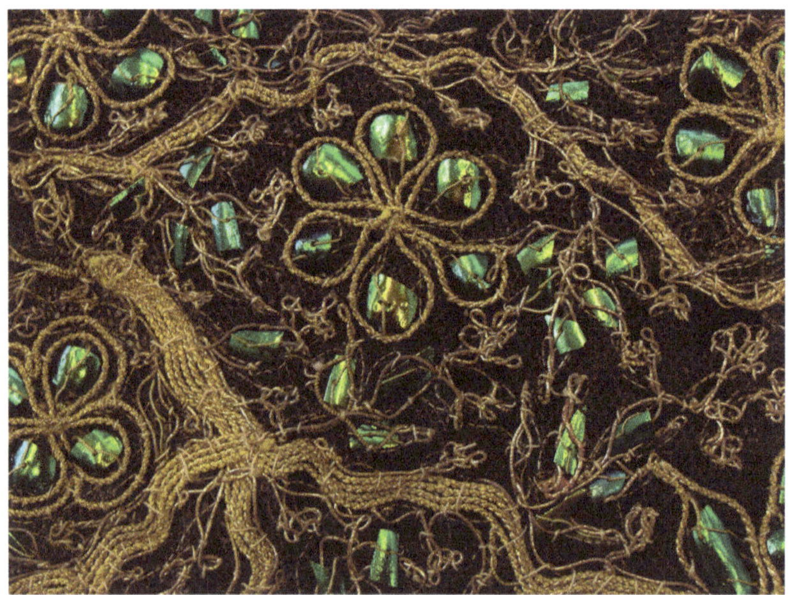

Figure 1. A textile ornamented with beetle wings.

[1] "'Beetle Wing Dress' for Lady Macbeth," *National Trust,* https://www.nationaltrustcollections.org.uk/object/1118839.1.

embroidered with hundreds of iridescent wings from the Far East, possessed the wild mystique of the jungle, the primordial allure of dangerous, creeping things.

With festoons of cloth of gold, Henry VIII and Francis I established a diplomatic encampment that would go down in history simply as The Field of the Cloth of Gold.[2] In today's textile industry the epithet would be an exaggeration: gleaming gold fabrics might

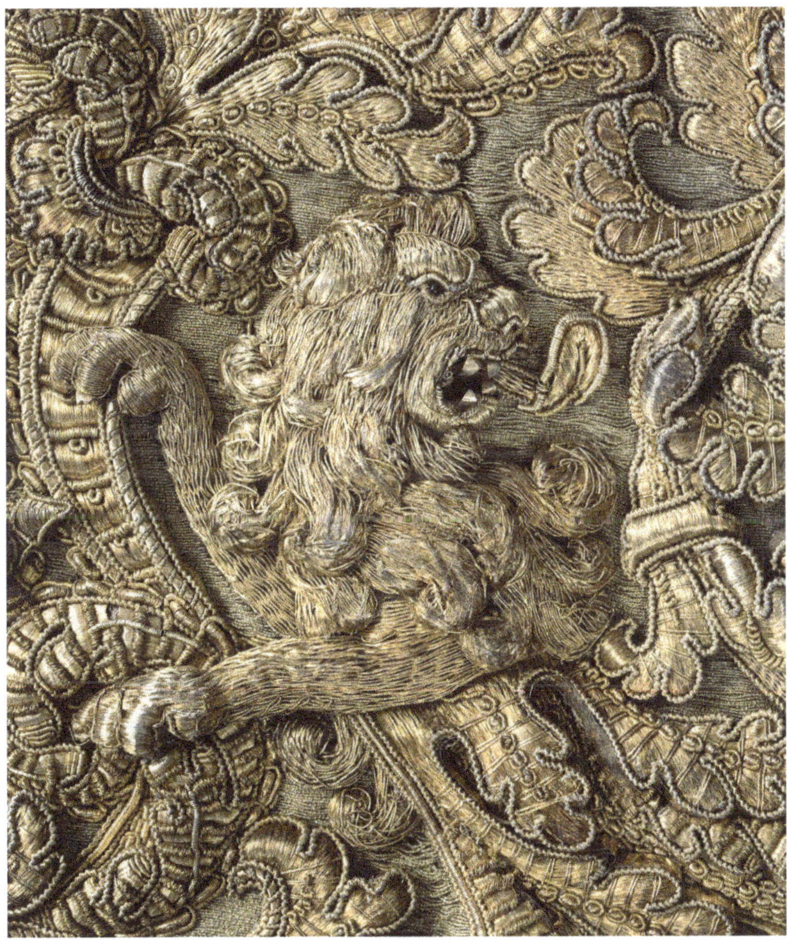

Figure 2. Lion motif in cloth of gold. Circa 1670.
(SOURCE: ROYAL ARMOURY MUSEUM, STOCKHOLM)

[2] Sean Cunningham, "The Field of the Cloth of Gold, 1520," *The National Archives,* June 9, 2020, https://blog.nationalarchives.gov.uk/the-field-of-the-cloth-of-gold-1520/.

look costly, but, in reality, they are woven with the cheapest polyester fibers. Not so, in that age before industry; the fabric of kings didn't just look like gold—it *was* gold.[3]

At a wedding dress design meeting, a young bride looked up from a swatch of mulberry silk and asked me incredulously, "Do you mean to say this was really made by little worms?" "Yes!" I assured her. "Only little worms could make something that beautiful."[4]

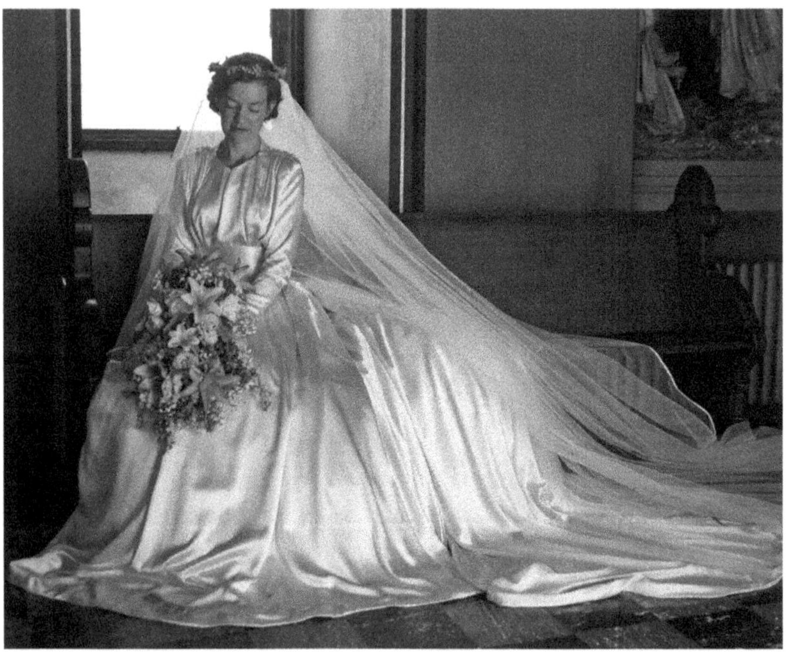

Figure 3. A bride in a homemade gown of silk crepe back satin. Fall 2023.
(PHOTO: ISABEL NOLAN)

[3] "Cloth of Gold," *V&A*, https://collections.vam.ac.uk/item/O130131/cloth-of-gold-unknown/.

[4] Silk appears well in still photos and film footage, but until one has felt it, handled it, been enrobed in it, one has not yet fully experienced its value. A silk crepe skirt fluttering around one's knees on a breezy day is astonishingly like the gentle currents of a cool, freshwater spring; running one's hand over silk duchesse satin is like stroking the wing of a dove; and the ripple of a silk charmeuse scarf makes one think, somewhat fantastically, of delectable liquid chocolate. Yes, silk is a *mirandum* no less than gemstones and pearls. Fallen humanity does not deserve what little of this precious fabric we have. The wonder is not that silk is costly, but, rather, that we, careless philistines that we've become, have even retained the art of producing it—that it, like so many other treasures, has not been entirely lost to us.

Each of the above episodes illustrates the ability of the world's natural materials to inspire wonder in the heart of man; and this wonder, it is important to note, is wholly distinct from environmental concerns. The dignitaries in The Field of the Cloth of Gold did not rejoice in that gleaming fabric because it was free of microplastics. Nor did the London gentry patronizing the Lyceum particularly care whether Lady Macbeth's dress was biodegradable. Even today, when environmental concerns are a common topic of debate, the bride, delighting in her silk wedding satin, hardly does so because she's thinking of reducing landfills. And, though many a pragmatic bride may strive for some measure of comfort on her wedding day, very few choose silk over polyester merely for the natural fabric's moisture-wicking properties. One might suggest, then, that the question is purely one of aesthetics: silk looks better than polyester. But while this is obvious to experts in textile design, it cannot be denied that textile engineers have developed such successful methods for synthesizing natural materials that often the differences are subtle. There is, it seems, an additional factor that gives natural materials their underlying appeal.

Despite their waning prominence in everyday life, natural fabrics still possess handles our minds can readily grasp. Whether we think of linen, cotton, wool, or silk, we call to mind familiar and largely pleasant images that smack of life, growth, and the touch of the human hand. If one does not know that linen comes from flax or hemp, one at least knows it comes from a plant. The same is true for cotton. Wool, the fabric of winter, seems a perfectly logical use of a sheep's thick, curly coat. And even silk, made by that fascinating process of a caterpillar's cocoon secretion, is, in the end, not so far beyond our imagination, perhaps due to every man's experience with the delicate threads of spider webs.

With synthetics, the case is not so clear. Consumers who bother to look at their clothing tags today will see an array of polymer names as dubious as the ingredients listed in small print on junk-food wrappers. Everyone has heard of polyester, nylon, acrylic, and spandex, but how many know what they are? To be told these materials come from a complex process by which fossil-fuel byproducts, through highly industrialized chemical reactions, become small bead-like pellets which may then be melted down into a slew of plastic products does not particularly illuminate matters. We think only of belching petroleum wells, white fluorescent factories, and robotic arms punching out now a bottle, now a shopping bag, now a dress to sell on Amazon.[5] We gain no appreciation for the materials themselves but only come away a little cowed by the colossal scale, complexity, and, if we're being frank, searing ugliness of it all.

An objector might hurry to say this is a problem of education then. Man must simply be taught the wonders of the technological world; he must be made to appreciate the chemical genius that has brought the world polyethylene terephthalate;[6] he must look closely at the industrial marvels housed in every Chinese factory. There have indeed been initiatives in this line, two notable examples being the television documentary series *How It's Made*, airing first in 2001 on Canada's Discovery Channel,[7] and, predating that, segments of *Mr. Rogers' Neighborhood* called "Factory Visits."[8] In such shows, mesmerizing video montages manage to make the jolting industrial system appear to glide away at its work, the screeching of machines muted and replaced by soft jazz piano accompaniment or stock "Science" background music.

But now as the generations who feasted on this glut of technological propaganda come of age, one might well ask: *Do* they wonder? Has their exposure to television screens airing the industrial processes of post-modernity awakened them, invigorated them, made them marvel at the gift of being alive? In reality, there is, in the confrontation of such systems, an enervating effect. Those fed such a diet most often come away apathetic, vaguely wondering why, in the face of so many well-oiled machines, man ought to try his hand at anything.[9]

[5] "Polyethylene terephthalate," *Britannica*, https://www.britannica.com/science/polyester.

[6] "PET—Manufacturing process of polyethylene terephthalate (PET)," *Valco*, https://www.valcogroup-valves.com/faq-2/manufacturing-process-polyethylene-terephtalate/.

[7] "How It's Made (a Titles & Air Dates Guide)," epguides.com, July 16, 2024, https://epguides.com/HowItsMade/.

[8] "Mr. Rogers on how crayons are made," https://www.youtube.com/watch?v=MWAhnVYUPZo.

[9] Seeing this, educators have scrambled to "give them the theory behind it!" As a result, every child with a pulse is hurried through a slew of STEM courses

It is not, then, a lack of technological understanding that prevents us from loving synthetics; it is simply that such artificial materials, clever as they may be, fail to touch our hearts or lift our minds to a higher plane. We cannot detect God's fingerprints in them. Being, as the labels tell us, "man-made," synthetics furnish a world where man would become his own god, a world like a horizontal tunnel that allows no upward ascent.

But it is precisely this upward ascent for which man was intended. Through the stewardship of creation that has its fulfilment in the sacramental life, man rises to meet his Creator and even to become like Him. "What is man that Thou art mindful of him? or the son of man that Thou visitest him?" the psalmist asks and then goes on to answer:

> Thou hast made him a little less than the angels, Thou hast crowned him with glory and honour: And hast set him over the works of Thy hands. Thou hast subjected all things under his feet, all sheep and oxen: moreover the beasts also of the fields. The birds of the air, and the fishes of the sea, that pass through the paths of the sea. (Psalm 8:5-9)

Man reaches this height—this status that is only a little less than the angels—by glorifying God through the sacramental life. The sacraments rely on the simplest elements of creation: fire, water, salt, oil, wheat, grapes, beeswax, and so on. These materials were created first and foremost for the sacraments. God did not institute Baptism and then decide to use water for it; He created water for Baptism.[10] He created wheat and grapes for the Eucharist, oil for sacramental anointing, gold for sacred vessels, bees and their wax for candles, spices for incense, flowers for the altar, linen for altar cloths, wool for the pallium, silk for priestly vestments, and so

---

in a desperate one-size-fits-all attempt to make a world of engineers. Some do well; some do poorly; but not a one is inspired with wonder, and, upon graduation, not a one could tell you what the shirt on his back is actually made of. All of the attempts to "wow them" (the world's version of wonder and awe) with technology have largely resulted in making them lazy. They have seen that the good things of life come from a black box full of intricate workings they'd rather not approach except, perhaps, via a lulling episode of *How It's Made*.

[10] Alexander Schmemann, *sacraments and Orthodoxy* (Herder and Herder, 1965).

on.[11] We often think of the Incarnation and all of its marvelous results (the establishment of the seven sacraments being the chief among them) as Our Lord's response to the fall, even as a general might hastily amend his strategy after a bitter defeat. But because God exists outside of time, and because He knew before all time that man would fall—that there would be an Immaculate Virgin, an Incarnation, sacraments, and liturgies—He created the universe with precisely this in mind.[12] Natural materials, in so far as they bring Christ to birth in us through sacramental liturgies, imitate the Blessed Virgin who gave birth to Christ in Bethlehem. They hasten to contribute their accompaniment to her joyful *Magnificat*.

Is it any wonder, then, that we who are meant to live by the sacraments would yearn for our lives and everything in them to also be a part of our Blessed Mother's canticle? The bride, delighting in her silk made from worms, senses His presence reaching through the exquisite perfection of His creation. The priest who desires cloth of real gold to adorn the liturgy, rather than the shining polyester that only apes gold, does so with the innate sense that he ought to offer Christ the best of the earth's riches just as the Magi did. Those kings of old did not come bearing polyester. The housewife spreading out a linen table cloth may think of the Eucharistic feast,

---

[11] "Those electric votive lights in Trastevere were more than stupid. They were an expression of a different sacramental order than that of the Church. They were simulations of a sacramental and as such mere simulacrums of the reality of fire, which is the true sacramental since it is one of those deeply symbolic 'elementals' of creation along with wood, stone, wind, food, and water. This is why, traditionally, churches and their altars are built of wood and stone, and the matter of the sacraments comes from wheat, grapes, water, and natural oils.... [There is a] sacramental difference between things that are grounded in natural elements which are then 'transposed' by human agency into things like wine and bread, and things which are purely synthetic and which are designed to imitate natural elements rather than to transpose them into a higher register." Larry Chapp, "How Christocentric and Spirit-filled are the synodal machinations?," *The Catholic World Report*, November 10, 2022, www.catholicworldreport.com/2022/11/10/how-christocentric-and-spirit-filled-are-the-synodal-machinations/.

[12] Chapp again: "The usual tack is to say that since water sustains biological life, it is an apt symbol for the impartation of divine life. He [Schmemann] affirms instead that God created water first and foremost with baptism in view, which is why God also decreed that water would also sustain biological life. The theological ordering is to view creation and bodiliness precisely through the lens of the Incarnation as its very reason for existing."

the linens of the altar, Veronica's veil, or the Holy Shroud.[13] And even the man in his simple wool suit may well think of sheep and Christ the Good Shepherd. This consciousness of the materials with which we surround ourselves, those that are in contact with our very flesh, profoundly shapes us. Either we are formed by the natural and its wealth of links to the life of God, or we are compromised by synthetics devoid of His fingerprints, devoid of beauty, and echoing with the world's dull groans of despair. We live either in a sacramental universe or in a synthetic one.[14]

Of course, there are those who would say this theology of materials goes too far. Natural materials might be preferable, they argue, but they are not actually as important as all that. But anyone who values the Church's traditional liturgy will understand that what man receives from the hand of God and learns through the five senses is immeasurable. The astonishing significance of materials in the path to heaven or hell is, in fact, a kind of scandal established by God Himself. In the sacraments we see this most starkly: the Eucharist comes to us only by the aid of wheat and grapes, temperamental fruits of the earth not even native to many climates. For Baptism, that great resurrection of the immortal human soul, we are dependent

---

[13] With his characteristic effusion, Romano Guardini has this insight on linen: "Good linen, strong-fibered and close-woven, is a costly material. It has the luster of fresh snow.... Linen has much to teach us about the nature of purity. Genuine linen is an exquisite material. Purity is not the product of rude force or found in company with harsh manners. Its strength comes of its fineness. Its orderliness is gentle. But linen is also extremely strong; it is no gossamer web to flutter in every breeze. In real purity there is nothing of that sickly quality that flies from life and wraps itself up in unreal dreams and ideals out of its reach. It has the red cheeks of the man who is glad to be alive and the firm grip of the hard fighter." *Sacred Signs* (Os Justi Press, 2025), 39–40.

[14] Regarding this topic, Peter Kwasniewski writes as follows: "The fabric made from natural things makes it more clear that man is a steward of the garden of creation, a cultivator of its fruits; he literally wears part of the world on his own skin, like a tree covered with bark, or an animal with its own fur. The kinship of man with the world and his kingship over it are strongly accentuated this way. When man invents a chemical that functions like a natural substance and then produces it in a factory, he is moving away from a humble and comforting dependency on given creatures and moving toward a more god-like role of creation. This is not a sin, but it puts man in a different relationship with the world—more distant, more imperious, and more pliable to his will." Private correspondence, 2023.

on something as humble as water. Here, by the greatness of God's providence, a bridge joins the natural world with the supernatural. This astounding collaboration of the material and spiritual is the miracle of every sacrament.

Recalling the usual non-spiritual arguments made in favor of natural fibers (i.e., biodegradability, greater comfort, greater aesthetic value), I reiterate that we should not deny the validity of any of them. However, to rely exclusively on those arguments is to miss the strongest argument of all: contact with natural materials is a fundamental aid to human salvation. This is undeniably the case when it comes to the sacraments, and it is the case to a lesser degree in every other aspect of life. Striving to fill the sanctuary with beautiful materials is the noblest of goals, but the quest cannot end there. The Lord did not make us for fragmented lives in which we worship one way and live another way. If human life is to consist of constant praise of God and not isolated flashes of worship confined to the celebrations of the sacraments, then we must promote and defend those countless quasi-sacramental moments when a great spiritual truth, a spark of beauty, or the sweetness of God's goodness come to us via the humblest of natural materials.[15] These moments push us to heaven like gusts of heady wind in our sails. They relieve us of the weary strain at the oars and let us rest for a moment, even fly. The absence of such moments acts as an opposing current, something that drains us, something that would make us drift to a hell of our own making.

Every moment of our lives at home or at school or at work should bear the marks of God's creative hand. Our clothing, together with the fabrics from which it is made, is vitally important because it goes with us everywhere, speaks to us constantly, tells us who we are. Our quest even today for linen, cotton, silk, or wool is not the faddish whim of silly "trad wives" but a rightly ordered instinct that reaches for things that silently speak of God. Even if, regrettably, natural materials pass today through industrial systems as harmful to the earth and culture as those which produce synthetic materials, the

---

[15] Hildebrand, *Aesthetics*, 1:211.

natural materials themselves cannot be robbed of the advantage of their origins and properties. They will always have greater ontological value than synthetics, and this is a truth the human soul can perceive.

Now, given its basis in the spiritual and sacramental realms, this argument in favor of natural materials is, admittedly, a difficult one to defend in a rationalistic system that denies the spiritual altogether. Nevertheless, it is the responsibility of believers to fight against anything that threatens human life, particularly the life of the soul. The rapidly increasing pervasiveness of synthetics coupled with the clothing industry's Fast Fashion paradigm[16] has all but destroyed the cotton, linen, wool, and silk markets in the span of a few decades. The onslaught has been virtually unremarked by Catholics. However, when it comes to another field of technological advances, that is, medicine, we have seen that certain Catholics have made great progress in promoting medical ethics and defending human life from conception to natural death. Thus, in a similar way, we need artists and philosophers to promote an artistic ethic that defends, first and foremost, the life of every human soul. In other words, the areas of materials and the arts in general must be viewed as domains subject to ethical standards. We must always ask the question: is what we're making going to bring harm to human souls, even indirectly or over a long period? Is it going to thwart the restoration of a culture in which human souls live, grow, and are saved?

If Catholics do not rise to the challenge, no one else will, simply because no one else can. Those without the Faith will never understand their deepest longing for natural creation and are therefore totally unprepared to defend it. Environmentalists are easily sidestepped by false promises and sham recycling initiatives. Aesthetes will be forever dismissed as snobbish and fastidious: "The average person can't really tell the difference between silk and polyester anyway," critics say. And even arguments for comfort such as the great breathability of linen are made less relevant by the recent improvements of moisture-wicking technologies in synthetics. In

---

[16] Alex Crumbie, "What is fast fashion and why is it a problem?," *Ethical Consumer*, April 9, 2024, https://www.ethicalconsumer.org/fashion-clothing/what-fast-fashion-why-it-problem.

short, there are many reasons for which the man without faith may finally suppress his longings for the natural. The question we Catholics must ask ourselves is what excuse do *we* have to suppress them? Or what will we tell such a man when he does come to know God? How will we justify ourselves for letting those materials that bear His fingerprints disappear from our lives? It falls squarely on believers, those already basking in the blazing light of the Faith, with access to the Church's knowledge stored up over the centuries, to apply every gift they have to protecting the world God created and inscribed with His Holy Name.

THINGS WE CAN DO RIGHT NOW

1. *Priests should discontinue the use of synthetic fabrics in every part of their ministry.* Vestments should be silk. Altar cloths, albs, and surplices: linen. Cassocks, from the oldest minister down to the smallest altar boy: 100% wool or wool blended with some other natural material (e.g., a wool-silk blend or a wool-cotton blend). Altar carpets: wool or silk. Lace: cotton or linen. Festive draperies and banners: silk (cotton and linen for outdoor use). It is far better to have no fabric than synthetic fabric. You may go years without a banner, an antependium, or some other desired adornment, and this is all right. Allow the faithful to live the virtue of holy poverty. Rather than rushing to a manufacturer of cheap religious goods to purchase a synthetic banner with an AI-generated image, explain to the faithful why you're taking the time to procure something better. Ask the faithful to donate funds or artistic talent to aid in the making of something worthy and beautiful. It will take time, and that is good. The spirit of hurry, that compulsion to plug every lack with the fastest, cheapest, and the easiest, is antithetical to Catholic life.

2. *The faithful should consider how they clothe themselves and their children for the sacraments.* A cotton or linen baptismal gown, however plain, is superior to a polyester one. Likewise for First Communion, Confirmation, and wedding dresses. Though ornamentation is understandably appealing, we must seek honest ornamentation that has not sacrificed material integrity and dignity for cheap frills. We are

so used to tawdry sacramental gowns that we hardly remember the beauty of real ornamentation: e.g., cotton needle lace, painstaking pintucks, seed pearls lovingly applied by the human hand. The average home seamstress is capable of making a wedding gown. With the money she saves on labor, she may easily afford many yards of silk.

3. *In everyday life, we should, wherever possible, phase out all synthetics.* Bedsheets and table cloths should be cotton or linen. Window drapes may be any natural material. Better to have no carpet than a synthetic one. Finally, with regard to clothing, better to have a few natural items than many synthetic ones. This is the cardinal rule.

6

Learning from
the Valiant Woman

AVING NOW CONSIDERED ART principles, beauty versus elegance, and the benefits of natural materials, readers may well be wondering about the effort involved in pursuing these ideals. As I have pointed out, we do not live in a world that encourages our pursuit of beauty. In fact, the clothing market's offerings are so inferior that many of us have given up the hope of ever really liking our clothing. To find things that fit and look well, all while feeding and educating our children, is an uphill battle to say the least.

Many Catholic women, desiring better dress for themselves and their families, balk at the quest for what seems to them almost mythical articles of clothing. For instance, a woman desiring a graceful skirt to wear when running errands on cold winter days searches superstores and department stores, Amazon and Goodwill. She finds a few thin polyester maxiskirts in garish stripes or hibiscus prints, but the graceful wool circle skirt or the elegant tweed A-line of her dreams utterly eludes her. After many hours of fruitless hunting, she despairs and forces herself to come to grips with yet another bleak winter of jeans and sweat pants.

The situation is more or less the same in all seasons and contexts of life. Whether dressing for errands or a wedding, the moment a woman decides to seek clothing of better materials and more beautiful design than the standard fare, she comes face to face with the glaring reality that, in today's society, there is no easy way to acquire such clothing. At this grim realization, she shakes her head sadly and leaves off her quest. She does not feel justified in putting any more time into the matter.

But I argue that she *is* justified in putting time into the matter. She need not think she acts on a frivolous whim. The instinct that urges her to look for something better, no matter how hopeless the quest may seem, is most certainly a good one. As I have argued in chapter 2, conformity to "normal" dress is not a neutral act—at least, not in the present day. It invariably means conforming to ugliness and often outright immodesty.

Although all souls claim membership in the mystical body of Christ, women particularly enjoy the privilege of embodying the Church (who is feminine, the mystical bride of Christ) and symbolizing her very essence.[1] This fact, rather than daunting women, should renew their zeal and encourage them to take up the quest once again. One has only to look at the Book of Proverbs' Valiant Woman to see that the acquisition of clothing for herself and her household takes up a good deal of her time:

> She hath sought wool and flax, and hath wrought by the counsel of her hands.... She hath put out her hand to strong things, and her fingers have taken hold of the spindle.... She shall not fear for her house in the cold of snow: for all her domestics are clothed in double garments. She hath made herself clothing of tapestry: fine linen, and purple her covering.... She hath made fine linen and sold it, and delivered a girdle to the Canaanite. (Proverbs 31:13, 19, 21, 22, 24)

This passage appears in the traditional sanctoral cycle for most non-virgin, non-martyr female saints, e.g., St. Anne, the mother of Our Lady. Its literal interpretation highlights the human, and very specifically feminine, solicitude of these saints and may serve

---

[1] Edith Stein, *Essays on Woman*, trans. Freda Mary Oben (ICS Publications, 2010), 237. "Thus woman achieves a particular organic position in the Church; and lastly, she is called upon to embody in her highest and purest development the essence of the Church—to be its symbol." See also Peter Kwasniewski, *Ministers of Christ* (Crisis Publications, 2021), 177–78.

to encourage all women seeking to bring beauty to everyday life. Edith Stein (St. Teresa Benedicta of the Cross) wrote: "Part of her [woman's] natural feminine concern for the right development of the beings surrounding her involves the creation of an ambience, the order and beauty conducive to their development."[2] Needless to say, clothing is a fundamental part of this ambience and order of beauty.

Of course, the structure of society today with its industrialization, mass production systems, and consumerism prevents a significant resumption of the ancient crafts practiced by the Valiant Woman. For instance, it is unlikely that many women will take up spinning or weaving at this stage in history. How, then, does the passage on the Valiant Woman speak to women in the present day?

In the literal sense, it shows that, even in the present day, women can, and should, devote *time* to the acquisition of clothing for themselves and their households.[3] Whether our garments are ugly or beautiful, clothing ourselves will always require some amount of time. The acquisition of beautiful clothing may have a learning curve that at first demands of us a little more time, but the learning curve can be surmounted. After some practice, women may find that, as a result of the online shopping they undertake (with niche retailers producing clothes not in the mainstream market), they actually *save* time. They no longer stand in dressing rooms at Dillard's or wait in lines at Walmart. They just measure themselves, review size charts, and click to purchase.[4]

Certain online retailers, though little known, often produce better clothing than expensive department stores.[5] Thrift stores too will sometimes have pieces of good quality, though women must be willing to spend time searching through the racks in order to find these

---

[2] Stein, *Essays on Woman*, 78.

[3] For a commentary that deals largely with the allegorical reading of this text, see Albert the Great, *The Valiant Woman*, trans. Benedict Ashley O.P. and Dominic Holtz O.P. (New Priory Press, 2013).

[4] Although the lack of the human element in online shopping is certainly regrettable, it must be accepted (like so many problems in post-modernity). One can hope that, with an increase in demand for beautiful clothing, the market may provide once again traditional brick-and-mortar shops in which customers may interact with those who produce their clothing.

[5] Some promising examples are listed in the Appendix.

hidden treasures. The task is to despoil the Egyptians, but only so long as the Egyptians are actually worth despoiling.[6]

Finally, those women who sew must prioritize the cultivation of this craft and seek to pass it on to their daughters. In this way, they will be armed with the ability to modify ready-made clothing to make it more modest or more beautiful; or, home seamstresses may make artistically successful garments from scratch. I know a woman who sewed a lovely maternity dress for herself using a bed sheet from a thrift store and a hundred-dollar sewing machine. In another case of home-sewing success, a young girl turned a backless prom dress found at a thrift store into a modest ball gown. Neither is a professional seamstress but both were willing to devote a little time and their God-given creativity to the art of dress.

INVESTING

In Catholic circles where true devotion and large families abound, one often encounters women unaccustomed to paying more than twenty dollars for any article of clothing. They may have grown up with older sisters and worn hand-me-downs their entire childhood, and now, raising families of their own, they strive to save every penny in order to keep food on the table. They might wish they could find better clothing for themselves and their families, but it seems to them unpardonably reckless to pay one hundred dollars for a skirt from an online boutique when they can obtain one for ten dollars at a thrift store.

Here I would like to emphasize that, although it has become a cliché, the maxim "quality over quantity" certainly applies. One beautiful skirt is better than ten ugly ones. The idea that one must wear something different every day is born from industrialization and is only made sustainable by shoddy manufacturing techniques and the use of synthetic fibers. It is far better to invest in fewer articles of higher-quality clothing, as these garments will not only achieve greater artistic success but also stand the test of time.

[6] For a valuable summary of the concept of "despoiling the Egyptians," see Peter Thomas Elliott, "Plundering Egyptian Gold: Christianity and Culture," Gonzaga Socratic Club, Friday, March 21, 2014, http://guweb2.gonzaga.edu/faculty/calhoun/socratic/Elliott_PlunderingEgyptianGold.pdf.

Additionally, frugal women might see this matter differently if they recognize that a woman who seeks beautiful clothing for herself and her household seeks their spiritual nourishment just as much as their physical protection from the elements. Man does not live by bread alone but requires the spiritual food and profound sense of repose which beauty in everyday life invariably brings.[7]

Clothing is also a powerful pedagogical tool. As the part of the material world that comes in constant direct contact with our bodies, it has profound power to teach us incarnate beings who we are. In a 1960 letter concerning dress, Cardinal Siri guides his readers with fatherly wisdom: "Since the world began, the clothing a person wears so determines and conditions gestures, attitudes and behavior, that clothing comes to impose, from the outside, a particular frame of mind."[8]

This observation cannot be overemphasized: clothing has the power to shape the mind. The secular world, driven by evil forces, certainly uses this reality to its advantage. Unfortunately, most of today's Catholics have yet to do the same. Instead of clothing that speaks the lies of sensualism, "gender-neutrality," and dystopian utility, Catholic women *could* wear clothing that helps them understand themselves in the eyes of God: graceful skirts and dresses—not impractical but not utilitarian either. Needless to say, tawdry, ugly, or immodest clothing clashes with the value and beauty of the wearer and says, "You aren't worth anything better."

When it comes to educating children through clothing, a little girl given a costly wardrobe will, of course, become spoiled if her parents fail to teach her gratitude and proper stewardship of this possession. But a girl given nothing but cheap, ugly clothing will be spoiled in a different way. She will not develop a proper view of her own dignity in the sight of God. Her clothing will make it difficult for her to realize her own ontological beauty. And she will not learn how to practice the art of dress successfully because, like a painter with runny paints, her defective materials will impede her

---

[7] Przybyszewski, *Lost Art of Dress*, xii.
[8] Giuseppe Cardinal Siri, *Christian Fashion in the Teaching of the Church*, ed. Virginia Coda Nunziante, trans. Brendan Young (Calx Mariae Publishing, 2022), 99.

ability to create something beautiful, leaving her tired and frustrated. It is vital, then, for parents, the primary educators of their children, and for all Christians, bound to speak the truth in word and act, to consider the message their clothing conveys.

Finally, viewing the family circle from without, one must acknowledge that the overall beauty that emanates from a large Catholic family holds greatest sway when all members are clothed well. In such a case, the visible beauty of their outward appearance produces a perfect harmony with the note of ontological beauty struck by their family unity. They have, so to speak, dressed the part. In the prevailing discord of today's world that has grown to accept family strife as normal (e.g., bickering spouses, disrespectful children, selfishness, laziness, and so on), it is little wonder that the clothing worn by families so deficient in charity usually reflects their moral discord. The well-dressed family who wears ordered clothing to reflect ordered souls stands like an abundant oasis in a barren desert. They bring the food of hope to all who see them. One can even go so far as to say that they reflect a spark of the beautiful and loving exchange of the Triune God. For this reason, to invest money into better clothing is actually an act of generosity, a work of mercy, in imitation of the Valiant Woman who "hath opened her hand to the needy, and stretched out her hands to the poor" (Proverbs 31:20).

LAUGHING IN THE LATTER DAY

In all approaches to the restoration of Christian culture, one must face the reality of the Cross. For all the beauty of sunlight shining on white linen, of ribbons fluttering in the wind, of young girls in pastel dresses like so many flowers in a field, one must toil like the Valiant Woman who "rises in the night," and this may often seem a thankless task. Clothing ordered online will not always fit as expected; things will get dirty, wrinkled, or not deliver the desired effect. There will be disappointments and setbacks and one may well ask whether the constant effort is worthwhile after all.

However, we read that the Valiant Woman "shall laugh in the latter day." Why does she laugh? What makes her so triumphant?

St. Albert the Great explains her laughter as springing from her faith in an eternal reward.[9] Everything then—tedious online shopping, hours at the sewing machine, the daunting task of ironing linen, the incessant work of stain removal—can become acts of faith for the woman who seeks the glorification of God.

The more trying the task, the more elusive the earthly gain, the more she can trust in heavenly victory. She who has persevered in her labors to raise the minds of men to heaven by the humble means available to her will herself be raised to the face of God; then she will labor no more but will rest forever, clothed in His infinite beauty.

[9] Albert, *The Valiant Woman*, 245–46.

7

Learning from Religious Sisters

May the Lord clothe me with the new man who,
according to God, is created in justice and truth.
(Prayer said by contemplative religious sisters
upon taking the habit each morning)

MOST WOMEN DESIRE TO DRESS more beautifully, but most balk at the prospect of standing out in the crowd. The desire to act in accord with our neighbors' ways of doing things is, after all, deeply ingrained in human nature. One hears all the time from women, wishing to elevate their dress but feeling the constraints of their environments, the worried question, "You don't think it's too much?" Some women even go so far as to interpret the simplicity in dress recommended by many saints as a recommendation to fall in with our current day's pervasive athleisure trend.[1]

But what is simplicity? Is post-modern dress really simple? Simplicity, as described by Webster, is to be "uncomplicated," "free from guile," and "direct in expression."[2] This definition corresponds with Aquinas' discourse on the divine simplicity of God and highlights the

---

[1] Notable examples of saints on dress being St. Paul (1 Timothy 2:9), St. Thomas Aquinas (*Summa theologiae*, II-II, Q. 169, art. 1), and St. Francis de Sales (*Introduction to the Devout Life*, ch. 25).

[2] "Simplicity," *Merriam-Webster*, https://www.merriam-webster.com/dictionary/simplicity.

relationship of simplicity to honesty and truth.[3] To dress simply is to dress honestly, that is, to express the truth in one's visible appearance.

Clinging T-shirts, yoga pants, and jeans call so much attention to specific areas of a woman's body that they detract from her own personality (as expressed in her face) and deny the presence of her immortal soul. On the other hand, baggy versions of the aforementioned speak so strongly of slovenliness, utility, and animal comfort that they contradict the ordered beauty of the human body and the eternal destiny of the soul. In short, whether clingy or baggy, erotic or unisex, most current modes of dress deny the truth about who and what human beings actually are and therefore lack simplicity.

For a woman to speak the truth through her attire, she must dress with femininity, order, and grace. In this practice, she discovers true simplicity and follows ranks of female saints who have gone before her. However, where most saints enjoyed cultural climates with sure customs that promoted beauty suited to each class and state in life, modern women find themselves in societal anarchy that only ever promotes ugliness. Women must now rediscover, re-assemble, and create anew what in previous generations was handed from mother to daughter as a matter of course.

Since there are currently very few women willing to commit themselves to this task, those who do will inevitably stand out. It's not that their clothing will be unnatural or outlandish—on the contrary, it will be much more natural and more distinctively human than anything seen in the mainstream today. Nevertheless, clothing that speaks the truth will turn heads as a result of its striking rarity. Before the fall of Christendom, no one would fawn over a wool circle skirt or stop to exclaim over a straw hat. Now the wearer of such articles finds herself accosted by both admirers and critics. It is this attention that gives well-meaning women pause. They do not wish to attract attention, to be celebrities at the grocery store, or to have covetous friends whisper behind their backs, "Who does she think she is?" But should we abandon the beauty of true simplicity in the name of self-effacement?

3 Thomas Aquinas, *Summa theologiae*, trans. Laurence Shapcote, O.P. (Aquinas Institute, Inc., 2012–2018), I, Q. 3, art. 1.

Somewhat surprisingly, the answer may be found in a short consideration of nuns and religious sisters. In the newer religious houses, where love of tradition prevails, one finds examples par excellence of young women seeking sanctity through self-effacement; they are anything but vain. And yet, in these same convents, one finds that meticulous care and substantial time are put into the design, production, and maintenance of a particular material item, the habit—that unmistakable sign of the religious that tends to stop traffic and draw attention everywhere it goes. Traditional sisters usually opt to source their own materials (I know one order that uses a high-quality wool blend typically used for police uniforms!). They then sew their habits either by hand or with simple sewing machines. These convents always have long lists of articles that need to be made or mended, and, before an investiture, when new novices receive the habit, the sewing rooms buzz with activity.

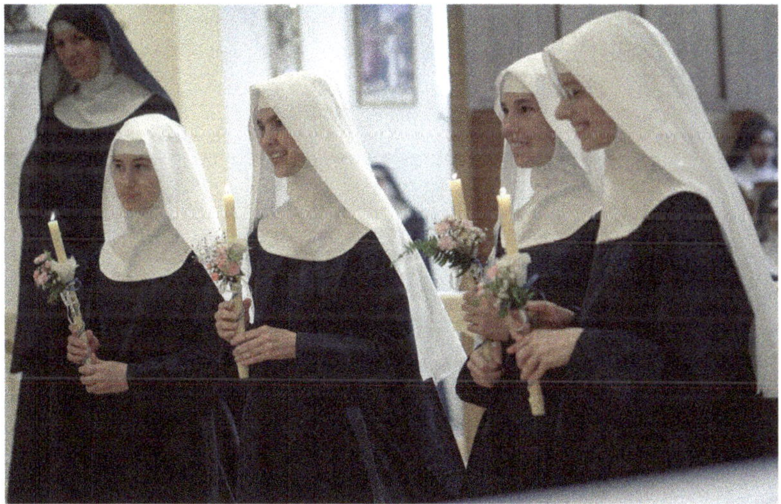

Figure 1. Benedictine novices. (PHOTO: TRACY DUNNE)

One could ask if it wouldn't be simpler and cheaper for the sisters to purchase ready-made secular uniforms of some kind. Better yet, why should they not blend in with society and just wear yoga pants and T-shirts like everyone else? Wouldn't that be most self-effacing of all? One has only to look to the disasters that befell religious houses following the Second Vatican Council to see that such misguided experiments have already been tried and, without exception, failed miserably.

The view that religious might embody higher virtue by dressing in ugly clothing is erroneous for three reasons. First, opting for the cheap and convenient does not embrace poverty but, rather, exhibits parsimony. Parsimony is never attractive. The Book of Sirach questions, "If a man is mean to himself, to whom will he be generous?" (Sirach 14:5) Second, the mass market does not produce anything with the beautiful and timeless quality that every religious habit ought to possess if it is to tell the truth about its wearer's vocation to live heaven on earth. Thus, every time sisters choose contemporary modes, they tell a lie. And finally, sisters who give up sewing work on the habit lose a profound source of nourishment in their lives, something that helps them through long fasts and hard labor, namely, the opportunity to channel that ultra-feminine propensity for making simple things beautiful. Mother Mary Francis provides an enchanting description of this in her classic *A Right to be Merry*:

> We do not paint things black where we could paint them white. We plant flowering tamarisk around our homemade incinerator because there is no reason why emptying the garbage should not be done with beauty and grace. We stitch our flour-sacking night guimpes with a precision and care that others might reserve for silk and satin. If poverty were thrust upon us, anything would perhaps be good enough. But we chose it, we espoused it. And we mean to clothe it in beauty.[4]

In the Middle Ages, nuns' habits resembled the dress of poor widows or married women of a lower class and thereby presented a chance for women to live all the more hiddenly, but now the very antiquity of their attire makes them stand out in contrast with the modes of post-modernity. Noticing this phenomenon in his historical work, *The Culture of Clothing*, Daniel Roche puts it thus:

> Both male and female ecclesiastical clothing constitutes a museum of ancient practices; the habit of the Daughters

---

[4] Mother Mary Francis P.C.C., *A Right to Be Merry* (Cluny Media, 2021), 44.

of Charity, a seventeenth-century congregation, was still, in the twentieth century, the female dress of the time of young Louis XIV; monks' robes take us even further back in time.[5]

To further understand these ideas, it is helpful to consider the following illuminated miniature which shows an array of beautiful medieval raiment and a small group of what looks like nuns:

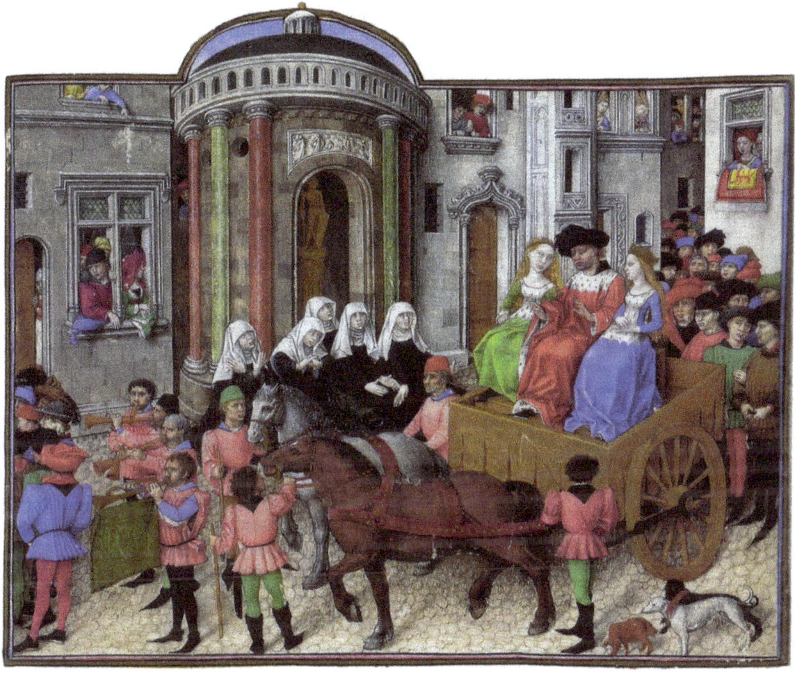

Figure 2. Poor widows resembling nuns. Barthélemy d'Eyck, "Triumphal Entry of Theseus into Athens." Illustration in Giovanni Boccaccio's *Il Teseída: Delle nozze d'Emília.* 1470.

In this miniature, the group of women who look like nuns are actually just a medieval depiction of poor widows. One sees how, next to the brilliant train of medieval dress, they only stand out for their relative sobriety. Today, this is not the case: religious sisters may still wear dark colors, but the timeless grace, the fabric quality, and the noble volume of their habits (i.e., the use of a greater yardage of fabric than most modern ensembles), all contribute to making them appear like they themselves are royalty from another age.

5 Roche, *The Culture of Clothing,* 74.

Compare religious habits with the contemporary street clothes:

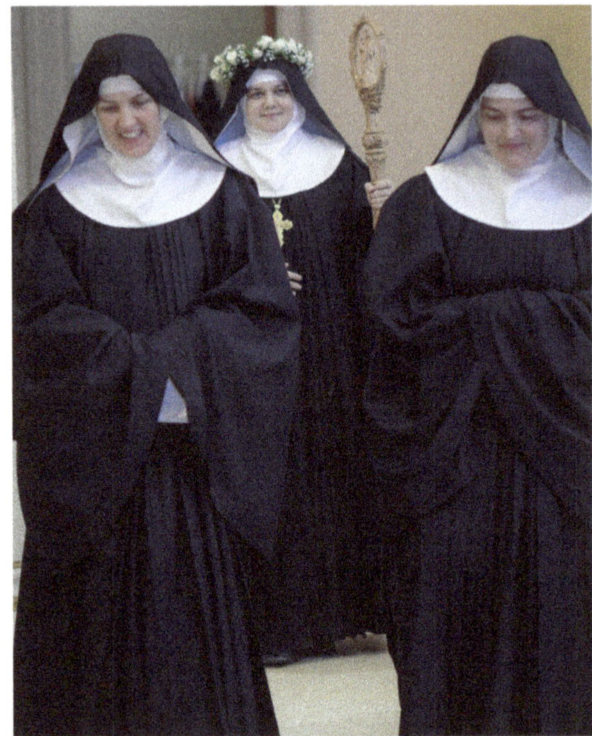

Figure 3. Enthronement of an Abbess (PHOTO: TRACY DUNNE)

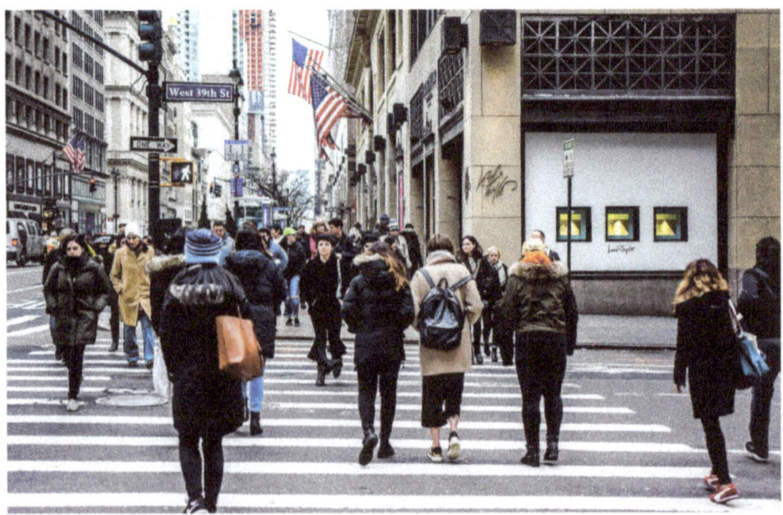

Figure 4. City pedestrians. (PHOTO: VLAD HILITANU)

One immediately sees that these Benedictine sisters would not appear poor, drab, or unremarkable in today's typical pedestrian traffic.

Thus, instead of blending into the crowd, religious sisters and nuns of today stand out like pearls that the receding tide has left behind. They do not balk at embracing those articles of clothing—namely, the floor-length tunic, the long veil, the universally flattering wimple, and the regal choir mantle—which truly sing the word of beauty; they embrace them as the surest way to express their status as brides of Christ Himself.

Are sisters in traditional habits trying to win admiration and praise? Far from it. But the humble rung of society into which they once blended has fallen away from the simple beauty of the Middle Ages to outright chaos and ugliness. While, in their humility, religious sisters might wish they did not draw so much admiration, they recognize that they cannot descend with society into false simplicity. Sisters who embrace tradition understand that, in one of those strange paradoxes of Divine Providence, the present sad state of dress makes the most humble, modest, and simple stand out like sparkling gemstones. Religious sisters embrace this as they embrace all parts of the mysterious Will of God, Who casts the mighty from their thrones and lifts up the lowly (Luke 1:52).

Our discussion would not be complete if I did not point out perhaps the most valuable lesson that the religious habit teaches us today: beauty is worth inconvenience. Many women abandon skirts, dresses, and all instances of what they consider an excess of fabric on the grounds that "it gets in the way." These same words rang out often during the dark years following the Council when religious orders jettisoned habits in favor of infamously unattractive lay garb. However, today orders that embrace tradition put up with all the inconvenience a long and full habit entails. Sisters smile when they realize their scapular (a long cloth rectangle worn front and back from head to toe) has been pinched in the car door and flapping along in the wind as they drive down the highway. They chuckle when their Rosary, worn at the waist, catches a doorknob and pulls them abruptly from their intended course. When it comes to keeping their wimples an immaculate white, sisters embrace this external challenge that reminds them so well of the serious business of keeping their souls pure. In short, the traditional habit represents a work of art that serves both a spiritual and practical purpose, but places the spiritual purpose first. This right ordering in clothing design is a profound lesson for all women.

Ironically, the convents in which the habit is most elaborate do not install mirrors. Appearances matter, but not for self-admiration. Rather, the habit wraps a sister in its folds and teaches her many great lessons while she is, so to speak, in the dark regarding her own appearance. If she looks beautiful, it is not for her own gain, but for the delight of Christ her spouse and for the edification of those around her.

Like religious sisters, Catholic women in the world must prioritize truth and beauty over normalcy and convenience. They must seek clothing that speaks of who they are, namely, daughters of Christ the King, types of the Church herself, and, married or not, spiritual mothers of immortal souls.[6] While their position in the world demands that they dress in a way that does not appear totally set apart from the world (only religious sisters have this great freedom), they may, on the other hand, legitimately adorn themselves in ways not allowable to women reserved for Christ alone. For example, they may have a greater variety of clothing, express joy through festive colors and trims, and enhance their forms with modest but flattering tailoring. Dressing beautifully, they will receive attention (either admiration or scorn), but this need not trouble them, if only, like their sisters in religion, they accept it as a mysterious part of Divine Providence acting in the present age.

---

[6] Alice von Hildebrand, "Spiritual Motherhood," *Plough*, May 8, 2022, originally published May 5, 2015, https://www.plough.com/en/topics/life/parenting/spiritual-motherhood.

8

On Men's Dress

IN A MUCH-NEEDED DIATRIBE ON THE "awfulness" of men's fashion, Sebastian Morello describes the other fathers at his children's school:

> Most of them looked like overgrown kids themselves. Typically, the fathers wore tracksuit bottoms—what in the U.S. are called "sweatpants"—and t-shirts, hooded jumpers, and trainers. Acceptable, perhaps, if you're off to a workout, but these men were off to the office. They looked awful. I would look upon these men, most of whom were middle-class and white-collar workers, and I'd think, "What a bunch of scruffs."[1]

Morello's description is too polite. He might have noted the ghastly effect such clothes produce when they encase the rolls of the overweight man. After all, athletic wear is now no longer the badge of honor chosen by the toned athlete; it is the only comfortable option for a body that cannot do without the merciful give of spandex. Nor does Morello point out the particular unattractiveness of the men who seem unaware that crossing the legs whilst wearing shorts reveals more than anyone ever wanted to see. Morello derides baseball caps plastered with logos such as NY for being worn incongruously by men the world over, but he does not take to task T-shirts printed with such edifying statements as "Am I perfect? No. But am I trying to be a better person? Also no." Or outright advertisements, such as one I once saw worn on a man at a Solemn Mass: "Mike's Junk

---

[1] Sebastian Morello, "On Not Looking Awful: The Three Sartorial Basics," *The European Conservative,* February 17, 2024, https://europeanconservative.com/articles/essay/on-not-looking-awful-the-three-sartorial-basics/.

Yard—Used Car Parts," with a phone number for anyone interested. Yes, Morello understates the case.

Writing particularly on the loss of hats in men's dress, Catholic writer Raymond J D. sounds forth the following lament:

> Along with our unfortunate love affair with sweatpants, leggings, and jeans for all occasions, our taste in hats has become abysmal. The baseball cap has taken over as the all-purpose non-winter hat. This, of course, is when one bothers to wear a hat at all.

And later:

> In brief, reclaiming nice hats is about more than nice hats; it's about reclaiming some semblance of ceremony or ritual, the sense that at least in some places and some circumstances, we shouldn't be too casual. There is a place for ceremony, in churches most of all, perhaps, but even in our daily lives. There is nothing stopping a priest from putting on a biretta any more than there is stopping an ordinary man from wearing a fedora, panama, trilby, or newsie. Why should our ordinary society be dominated by the cult of the casual?[2]

The noxious seep of the casual into every aspect of life is so at odds with the discipline and good stewardship of *cultus* that one must more accurately describe it as the anti-cult of the casual. There is, in all that slovenly dress described above, nothing cultivated.

And yet Morello himself declares he "does not much like suits" given their ideological origins as the garb of egalitarianism that chooses to be clad forever and always in gray. The rejection of masculine adornment marked a distinct and unprecedented rupture in clothing history, about which historian Daniel Roche writes the following:

> For many centuries, the two sexes were equal in the pursuit of refinement and decoration. From the Renaissance to the Enlightenment, men in refined milieus dressed both extravagantly and elaborately. But the eighteenth century saw the beginnings of a major historical rupture: the masculine

---

[2] Raymond J D., "In Defense of Nice Hats," *Gaudium Magazine*, May 2, 2022, https://www.gaudiummag.com/p/in-defense-of-nice-hats.

> renunciation of decoration, even of elegance, in favour of
> an austere appearance.[3]

Roche later describes how the wake of the French Revolution saw the emergence of the suits which have not varied much to our present day:

> In the case of men, a complete change of direction began
> with the adoption of trousers and coat, a certain tidiness
> and stiffness, an austerity of shape, fabric, and colour. Black
> triumphed. A colorless male society now presented itself in a
> dress which was *comme il faut*, proclaiming its attachment to
> notions of decency, correctness, effort, prudence and gravity.[4]

Many Catholics not keen on egalitarianism still hold the mistaken believe that austerity in men's dress is an appropriate expression of masculinity and complementarity. Women, they claim, are the blossoms, while men are the stems. It's a nice theory, and we make the best of it, grateful for anything that admits of an honest difference between the sexes; but it's not what was established in the beginning, and, frankly, it's not natural. We must recall that God made man and woman *both* in His image, which implies that man is imbued with the beauty of God just as much as woman, and man can be expected to reflect that beauty in a masculine way. Sacred Scripture is replete with references to male beauty, from Joseph's colorful coat (Genesis 37:3), to the Prodigal's welcome home with robe and ring (Luke 15:22), to the great Psalm 92 of Sunday Lauds: "Dominus regnavit, decorem indutus est."[5]

The suit, rare and welcome as it is today, has a few artistic failings. As has been noted, the colors are boring. We no longer notice how perfectly ludicrous it is for men to ponder carefully over the choice of gray, charcoal, black, navy, or (for the very bold indeed) cobalt. Commenting on this misfortune and urging women not to go down the same dull road, a dress manual in 1938 stated, "Men's fashions have cut the pageantry of the ballroom in half. It seems stupid for women to dispense of the rest of it."[6] Another dress consultant that same year praised the brilliantly colored suits sported by the

---

3 Roche, *The Culture of Clothing*, 38.   4 Roche, 58.
5 The Lord hath reigned, in beauty robed.
6 Cited in Przybyszewski, *Lost Art of Dress*, 255.

African men in Harlem, New York, who, by all accounts, cared little about what was *comme il faut*.[7]

Returning again to the historical rupture which caused this annihilation of color, Roche considers the effects of the Protestant Revolution which shook Europe before the fall of the *ancien régime* and no doubt contributed to the strength of the egalitarian ideology we see still manifested in dress (particularly men's dress) today. He provides an illuminating overview:

> Powerful models, those of reform and Puritanism, imposed their rigour on fashion. For a century, a strict style and sober colours conferred a symbolic sartorial colour on the whole of anti-Absolutist Europe, from Flanders to Geneva, from Prussia to England. To the polychrome magnificence of the Catholic aristocracies, displayed in the dazzling gold and silk of processions and festivals, contrasted the voluntary and quasi-republican effacement of the men of the reformed ethic.[8]

An analysis of the interplay between the Protestant Revolution and the French Revolution is beyond the scope of this chapter, but it does not take extensive historical training to see how the one fed aptly into the other. As for the United States, a country so rooted in English Puritanism (particularly in its historic centers of fashionable life on the East Coast), it is no surprise that the narrow palette of neutrals has prevailed down to the present day.

Of course, the lack of vivifying color in modern suits is only one problem, and perhaps the least problem. After all, a garment's color may be rectified merely by a change of fabric, or an update to the fabric dye. A far more essential flaw in the modern suit is its monotonous composition. Morello likens the trite matching of jacket and pants to pajamas. One might also think unfortunately of hospital scrubs or a prison jumpsuit.

Furthermore, the lines of the modern suit do relatively little for the wearer's figure. Rather than complementing the lines of nature, they superimpose crude, geometrical shapes over nature. One might

---

[7] Cited in Przybyszewski, 56.   [8] Roche, *The Culture of Clothing*, 58.

liken this to the effect of the Tesla truck: its bold, brutal lines are impressive, but they lack grace and bear a primitive quality, making one think of blocks of stone not yet refined by the artist's chisel, or, in a virtual world, three-dimensional models not yet fully rendered by the programmer's code. Like the Tesla truck, the man in a modern suit impresses us with dystopian austerity that is a far cry from beauty.

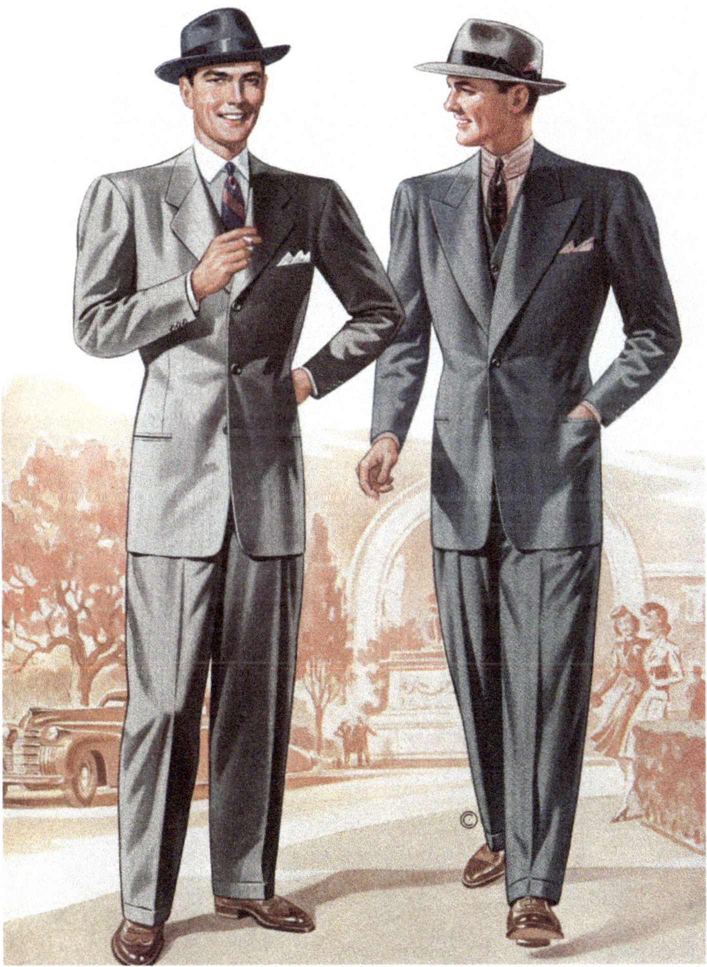

Figure 1. The modern suit. This fashion plate, dating from the 1940s, shows that the general characteristics of modern suits have not altered much since their birth in the nineteenth century. To mark changing details such as lapel width only proves the point that the artistic scope in men's modern dress is extremely limited. (SOURCE: *Newest Styles for Men,* 1940–41)

We have grown so accustomed to men's attire lacking grace that we now hardly know what we're missing. Only when one really considers modes of the past does one begin to comprehend the impoverishment of men's dress today. Take, for instance, the *justacorps* of the eighteenth century, cut all in graceful curves of ample, rich fabric in every possible hue, compared to the modern suit jacket, which is always just another gray block variant.

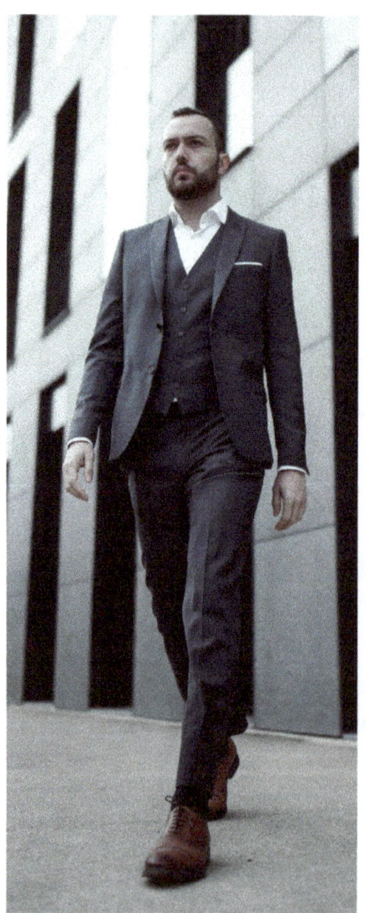

Figure 2. The dystopian gray effect of the modern suit.
(PHOTO: ALEXANDRE TROUVÉ)

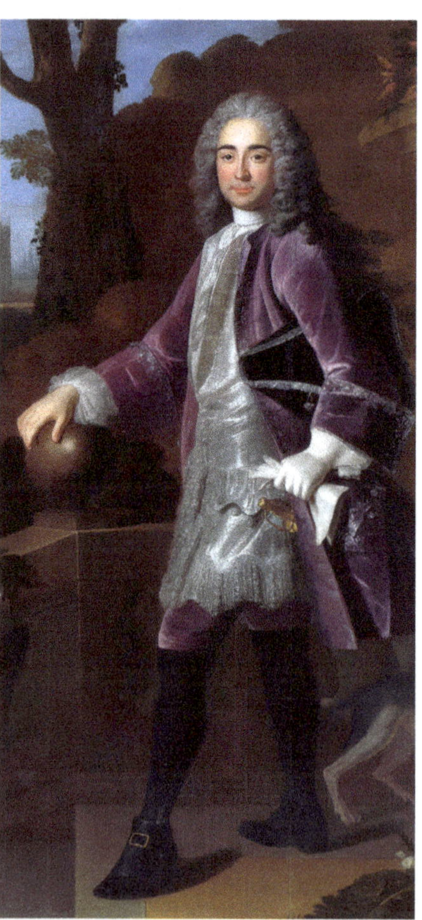

Figure 3. The beauty of the justacorps. Robert Gabriel Gence, "Jean-Joseph de Pons."

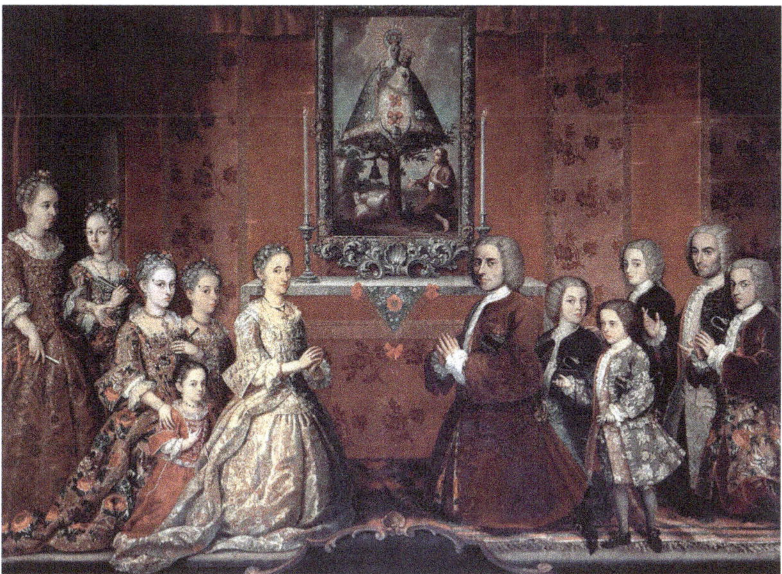

Figure 4. Portrait of Family Fagoaga Arozqueta. The Fagoaga Arozqueta family was an upper-class criollo family from Mexico City, New Spain. Note the beauty and ornamentation of the men's costumes, which still appear masculine and are quite distinct from the dress of the women.

The root of the problem is that the lines of the modern suit are not natural. They bear little relation to the man or any other part of nature. Everywhere one sees beautiful lines in art, one sees a connection with nature: the curved leg of an Empire sofa is a clear homage to the muscular leg of a lion; the slender arms of a candelabrum bear their flames like tree branches bearing blossoms and fruits; women's skirts, when they are beautiful, follow the lines of flowers, or waterfalls, or perhaps even the fanning tail of the peacock; even the more geometrical shapes of the classical style owe their genesis to the natural forms found in mathematical theory. One could go on with such examples. A man's boxy jacket and straight trouser leg resemble nothing. They are not supposed to resemble anything. Rather, they are supposed to serve a purpose and provide a good measure of comfort. If they are attractive, it is largely by accident—as if the gods of utility had carelessly allowed their artefacts some aesthetic appeal.

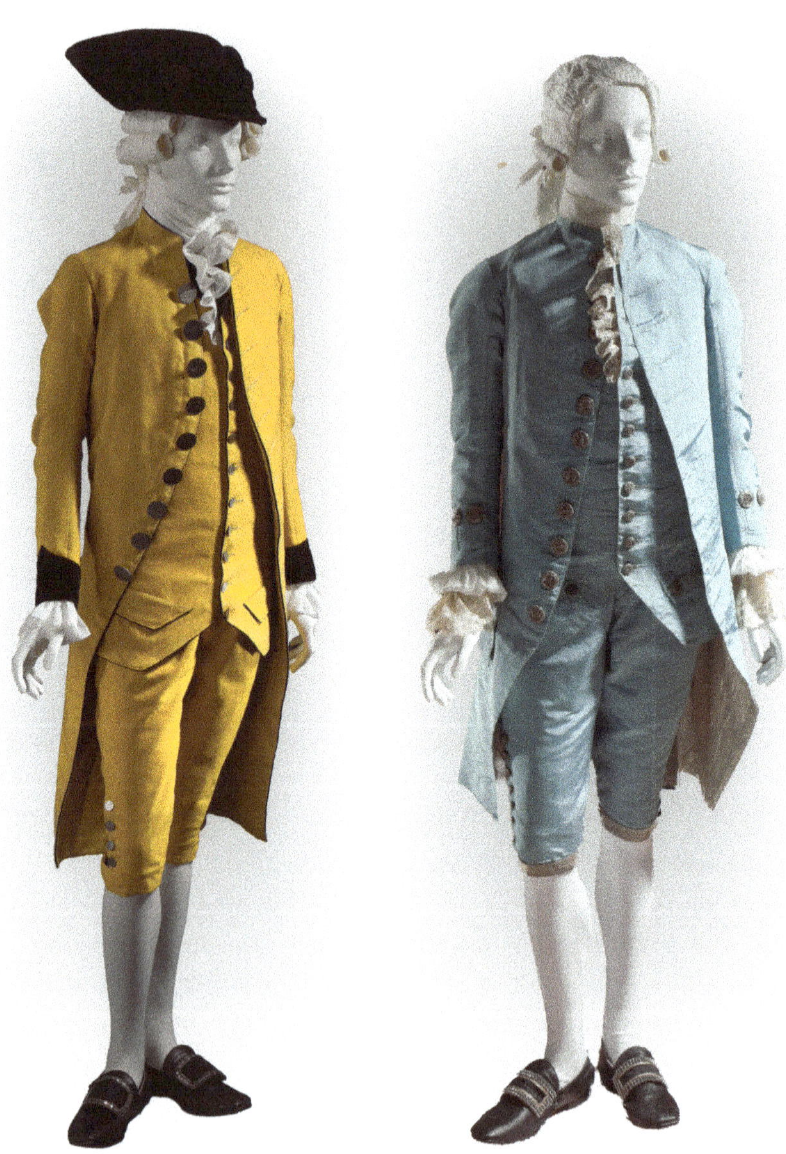

Figures 5 and 6. Examples of the splendid colors worn as a matter of course prior to the French Revolution.
(SOURCE: LOS ANGELES COUNTY MUSEUM OF ART)

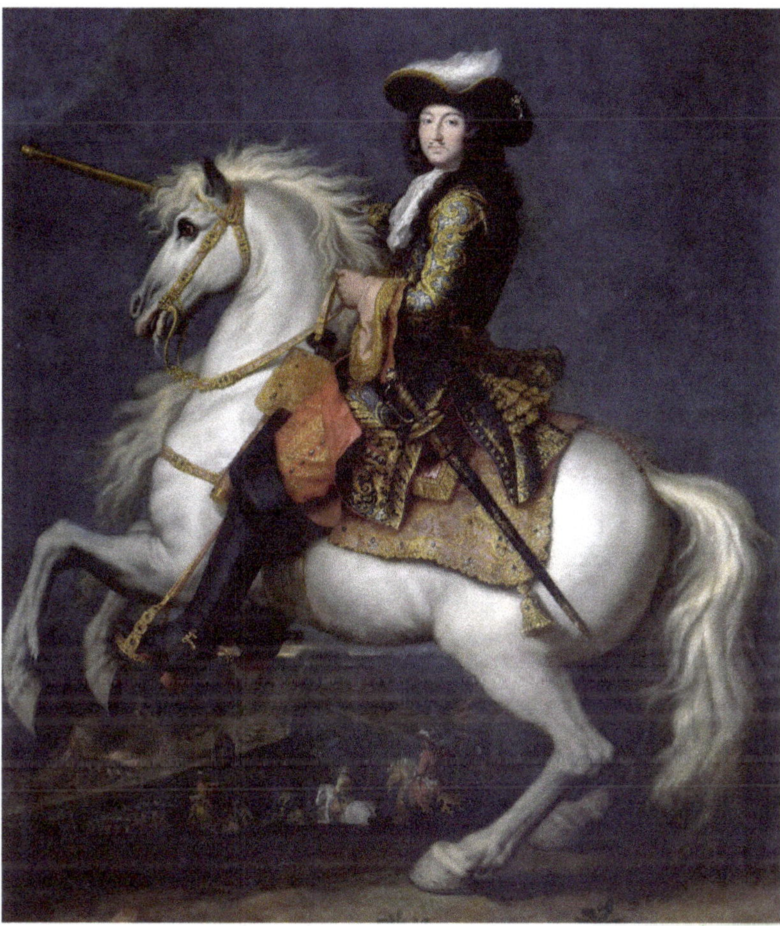

Figure 7. Equestrian portrait of Louis XIV victorious in battle, by René Antoine Houasse. Compare this to a contemporary portrait (available via a web search) of His Royal Highness The Prince of Wales.

Compare modern trousers—perhaps the most formless and unattractive garment ever devised for men—to knee breeches, worn by rich and poor alike well into the eighteenth century. Breeches allowed for a man to cover his legs modestly (with the addition of a waistcoat and jacket often reaching to the knees) in a way that would not obscure the stocking-clad calves of the man beneath. In her novel, *Adam Bede*, George Eliot describes this effect delightfully in the character of the prosperous farmer Mr. Poyser, who regards modern fashions with skepticism:

> Mr. Poyser was in his Sunday suit of drab [wool], with a red-and-green waistcoat, and a green watch-ribbon having a large cornelian seal attached, pendant like a plumb-line from that promontory where his watch-pocket was situated; a silk handkerchief of a yellow tone round his neck; and excellent grey ribbed stockings, knitted by Mrs. Poyser's own hand, setting off the proportions of his leg. Mr. Poyser had no reason to be ashamed of his leg, and suspected that the growing abuse of top-boots and other fashions tending to disguise the nether limbs had their origin in a pitiable degeneracy of the human calf.[9]

Of course, when promoting older, more beautiful modes of dress for men, one inevitably encounters lewd giggles and mutterings about "tights" and "codpieces." Indeed, there are some who seem to think that men did not discover how to dress decently until the nineteenth or twentieth centuries, as if everything that came before today's suit or athleisure ensemble was as good as dressing in drag. But within the array of garments worn by men throughout history, codpieces and hose possess a relatively small market share. Furthermore, it is important to note that hose were not usually form-fitting and were often worn with knee-length tunics over them. Codpieces began merely as practical elements of men's pants or armored suits. In combat, they functioned as protection exactly like today's athletic cup.[10]

---

[9] George Eliot, *Adam Bede* (Double, Page & Co., 1901), 191–92.

[10] Elizabeth Ellis, Kristina D. Suson, Janae Preece, Ronald Rabinowitz, "A Knight's Thrust: Was the Use of a Codpiece for Protection or for Exertion of Masculinity? An Evaluation through History and its Reemergence in Modern Times," *The International Journal of Urologic History*, vol. 3, no. 2 (Spring 2024): 20–26, https://ijuh.org/assets/pdfs/volume3/issue2/Ellis_Codpiece.pdf. The authors provide a good summary: "The armor used in the early Middle Ages was chain mail, which covered the neck, trunk, and upper arms and legs but failed to protect against blunt injury to the groin as weaponry became increasingly powerful. Full plate armor, developed by the 1300s, eventually included the codpiece, a small metal pouch to house the genitalia. In the late 1400s, however, codpieces appeared in civilian wear, modestly laced to men's stockings as upper body shirts and tunics became shorter. Codpieces quickly became more ostentatious and bulkier in an 'Arms Race' of masculinity, were soon ridiculed in contemporary satires including works by Shakespeare and Rabelais and inspired royal edicts limiting their use. However, the codpiece was used in the management of genital disease as well, as the bulky wraps and ointments used to treat endemic syphilis were thus more easily concealed.

They only became truly objectionable when they were exaggerated in the civilian sphere. Finally, lest we forget our own concessions to revealing garments in the present day, it must be admitted that hose and codpieces differ little in what they expose from the athletic pants of any NFL player.

Of course, in men's dress throughout history, we also see the tunic, the toga, the cassock, the kaftan, and many other garments more or less in the robe family. These, far from appearing effeminate, loaned their wearers a special dignity and masculine grace. Unlike knee breeches and stockings, which set off the strength of a man's calf, these garments concealed men's legs entirely, much like women's skirts—but with how different an effect! There is, in the solid fullness of a tunic, something primordially masculine, something fortitudinous and regal. Anyone who has compared the priestly clerical suit comprised of coat and trousers to the cassock and fascia will have noticed this.

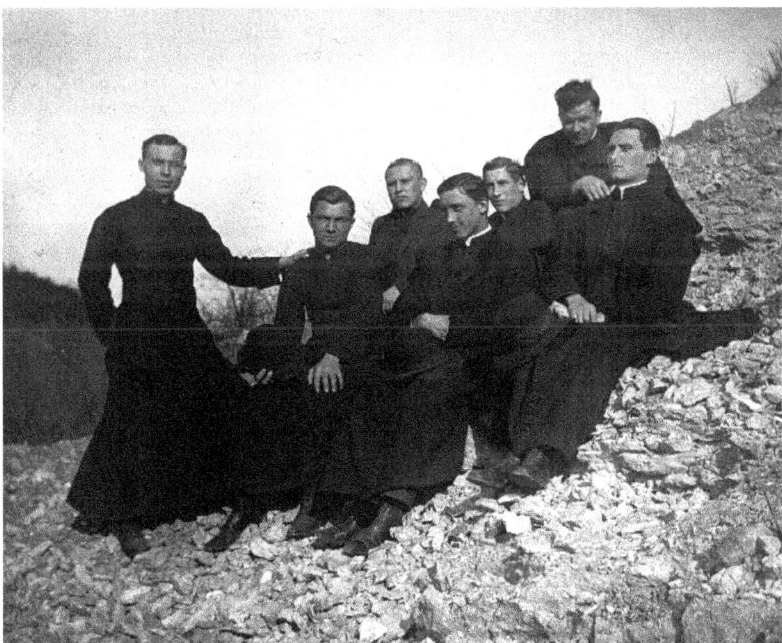

Figure 8. Priests or seminarians in 1935. Location unknown. One sees here that the cassock is far from effeminate.

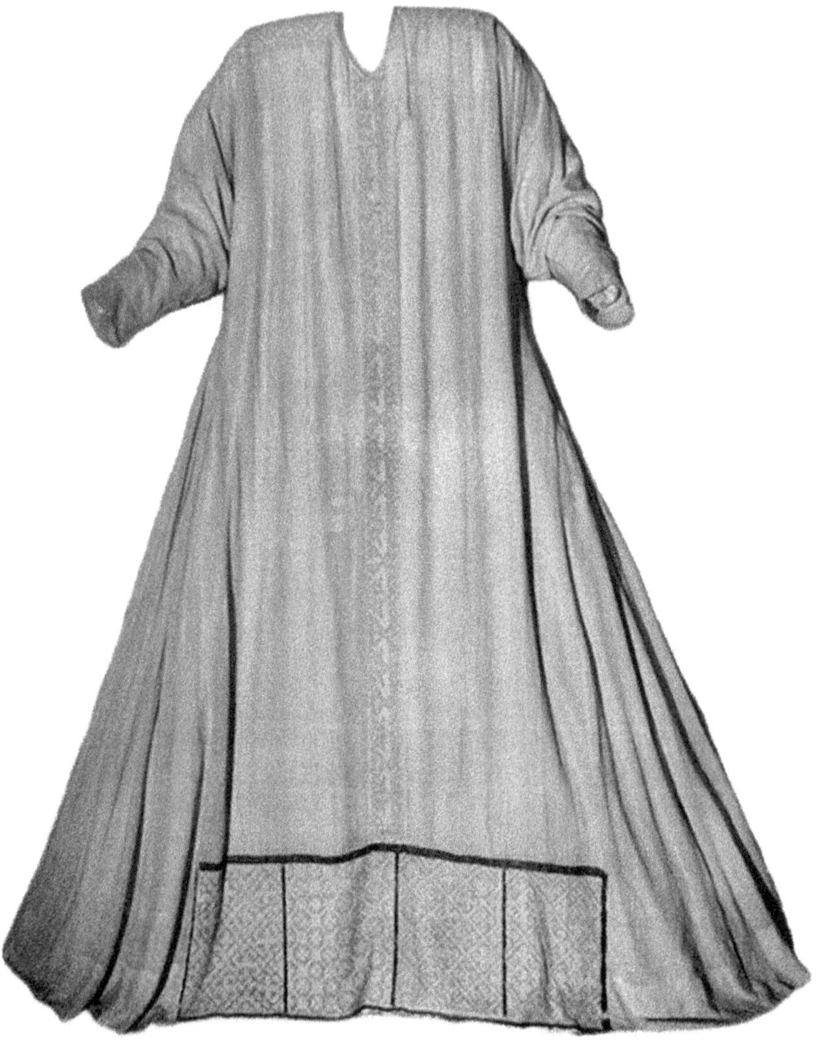

Figure 9. Linen alb circa 1240. Note the fullness of this alb made by none other than St. Clare of Assisi. The quantity of linen would give men pause today, but at that time, an abundance of fabric was recognized as a thing of beauty and appropriate for the priest acting *in persona Christi*. (PHOTO: JOHN PAUL SONNEN, *Liturgical Arts Journal*)

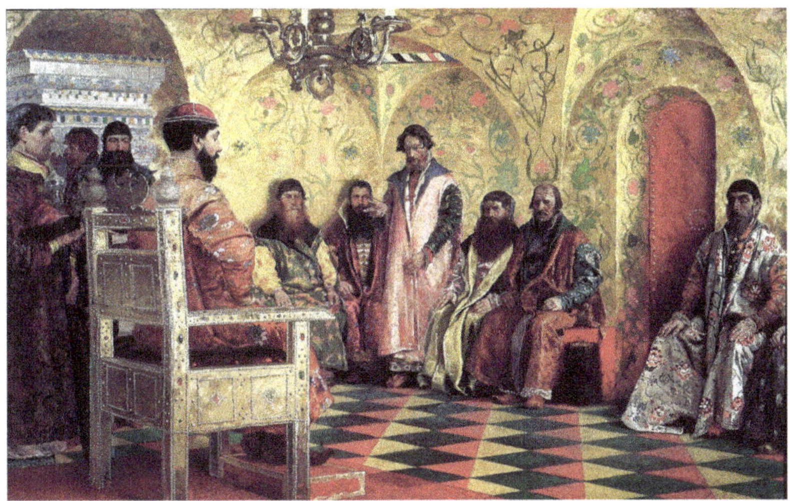

Figure 10. Russian nobles wearing kaftans. Andrei Petrovich Ryabushkin, "Tsar Mikhail Feodorovich at the session of the Boyar Duma." For more on the rich and beautiful history of the Russian kaftan, see Nicholas Kotar, "Everything You Need to Know about the Russian Kaftan," https://nicholaskotar.com/2016/03/10/russian-kaftan/.

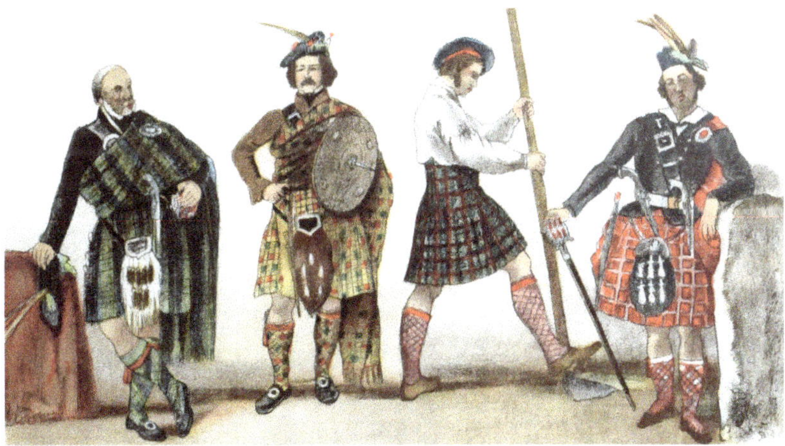

Figure 11. Very few are not aware of the wonderful plaid tartans worn in peace and war alike by the Scots. (SOURCE: ADOLF ROSENBERG AND EDUARD HEYCK, *Geschichte des Kostüms*)

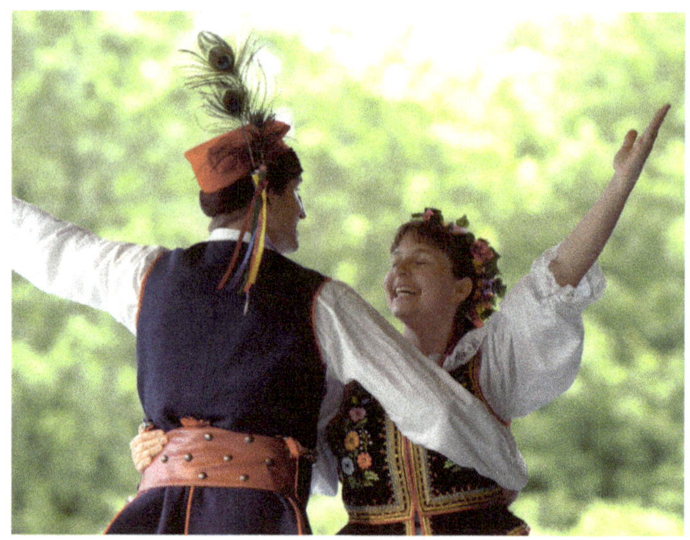

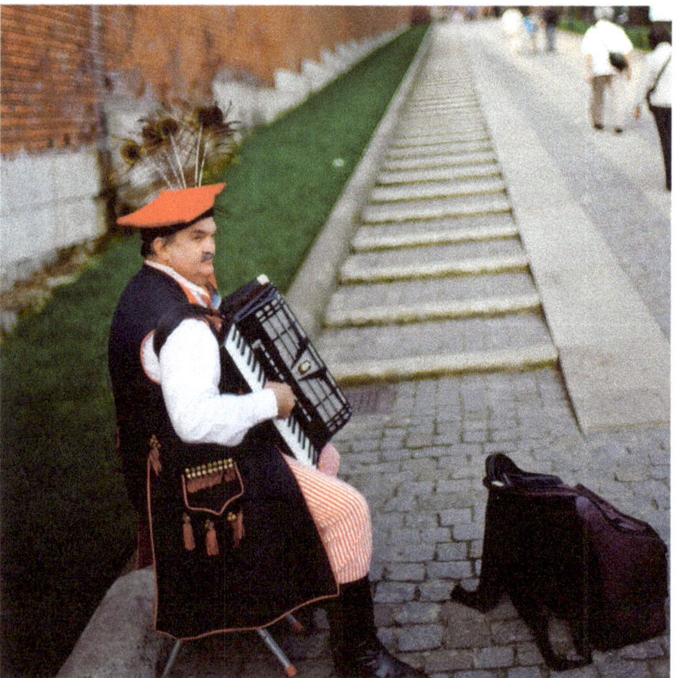

Figures 12 and 13. By the nineteenth century, festal garb for a Krakowian man consisted of a jewel-toned kaftan covered in tassels, candy-striped pantaloons, jaunty boots, and a crimson cap adorned with nothing less than peacock feathers.[11]

[11] For more information, read Anna Legierska, "Polish Folk Fashion: Pure Joy!," https://culture.pl/en/article/polish-folk-fashion-pure-joy.

The figures above are just a small sample from a vast array of styles bursting with color and beautiful, masculine lines worn by men, rich and poor, all throughout history until the modern day.

Commenting on dress in his *Aesthetics*, Dietrich von Hildebrand remarks that women's dress can sometimes still be called truly beautiful (versus merely pretty or elegant), but he is less generous toward men's dress:

> Men's clothing was often beautiful even as late as the Biedermeier period [1815–1848]; it was definitely beautiful above all in the Middle Ages, in the Renaissance, and in the Baroque and Rococo periods. But the prosaic long trousers which are customary today, and have been worn for the last 150 years, cannot be bearers of beauty.[12]

For Hildebrand, prose was the enemy of beauty. Prose dominates a post-industrial world where comfort and convenience are the only values; signs and symbols, the expressive function of clothing, that were part of that "poetry of life" so often lauded by Hildebrand, mean nothing. A prosaic world is dull and sterile and alarmingly desensitized to its own dreariness. Such a world, Hildebrand states, is terribly impoverished.[13]

But what can men do? Return to breeches or togas? Well, perhaps not quite yet. Poetic clothing requires poetic spaces, and in our world of suburbs and industrial parks and the soulless highway systems which must necessarily connect them, poetic spaces are tragically rare. Catholic churches, and only the very old ones, are just about the last bastions of poetic space in which any man, however poor,

---

[12] Hildebrand, *Aesthetics*, 1:400n1. Hildebrand makes two very interesting and somewhat humorous admissions later in this same footnote. First, he writes: "The necktie is the last remaining part of men's clothing which can be not only elegant, but even beautiful." And later, he gravely acknowledges artistic success achieved by hippies: "Today one can often observe a desire for men's clothing that is less plain and prosaic. This sometimes finds expression in the clothes of the 'hippies,' where the decisive thing is not only letting oneself go, that is, the protest of the bohemian against order and cleanliness, but also a meaningful longing to escape from the plainness of clothing and appearance. Their colorful clothes and long hair can be definitely beautiful."

[13] Hildebrand, 1:3.

may find refuge from the suffocating effects of prose. I often tell men if they'd like to dress beautifully in our present day, they have only one option: to become canons of the Institute of Christ the King. For everyone else, there's only modern elegance.

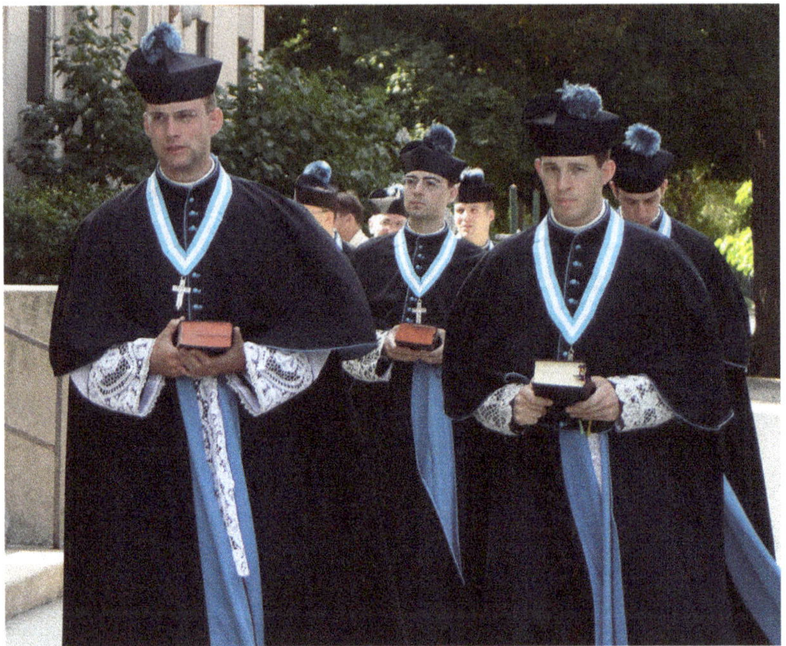

Figure 14. Canons of the Institute of Christ the King
Sovereign Priest. 2014. (PHOTO: XAVIER BOUDREAU)

And this brings us back to Morello, who, making concessions to the culture of suits because the athleisure alternative is so much worse, advises men to obtain a lapelled jacket, a collared shirt, and leather shoes with laces. Raymond J D. takes the message further in his apologia on hats: "With the range of options before us, for the priest and laymen, it is time to reclaim our heritage. It is time to strike a blow against the casual and the ugly. It is time to wear nicer hats."[14] Both writers emphasize that the choice to dress well is not the whim of eccentric fops but of men with enough sanity and healthy self-regard to refuse to go along with a world that has chosen to be "a bunch of scruffs."

[14] Raymond J D., "In Defense of Nice Hats."

In fact, this quest to rise above the ugly (for that is what the scruffs are) is a refusal to become a philistine, who, as Hildebrand writes, "pays homage to a pseudo-realism for which things are real only in the sense of a naked, austere usefulness. He [the philistine] regards everything else as a 'romantic' playing around, an illusion, a waste of time."[15] Philistines are the men who are quick to tell you the cost of a suit as—how it appears in their minds—an invincible reason not to buy one. Or, if they own a suit, they're even quicker to tell you how impossible the summer heat makes it to wear. Trapped in the smug delusion that appearances mean nothing, they are dead to the zeal that inspires the artist to make sacrifices for beauty. They feel not even the superficial urge to be admired.

Admittedly, the suit and its various dapper equivalents do not serve every occasion—to declare as much simply transfers the problem of universally casual dress to universally professional dress. Given human nature's primordial longings for variety, creativity, and personal distinction, the process by which men's dress has gradually narrowed to an almost uniform norm, and the rapid descent of that norm which can be noted from one day to the next, finds its explanation in the aggressive egalitarian battering of recent revolutions. In other words, it is not natural for men to wear the same thing in every place and on every occasion. As has already been stated, the suit is the most formal attire most men can pull off (like it or not) in the present day. What about informal occasions?

Short of a return to well-ordered hierarchical structures in which healthy diversity of dress may once again flourish, there is still one trick that will go a long way: men will seldom err if they stubbornly seek natural materials. Cotton, linen, wool, and silk will always appear interesting and distinct from one another, and each of these materials answers to particular demands made in men's lives: linen for hot summer leisure; cotton for hot summer labor; cotton flannel (light but warm) for work in the cold; knit wool for leisure in the cold. (Here, I cannot help but think of a photo of young Roger Scruton, sitting in his study of a winter day, pen in hand, clad in a wool cable knit

---

[15] Hildebrand, 1:219.

sweater.) Finally, silk or the ingenious blend of wool and silk answer, as they have always done, to occasions of formality and festivity.

One may ask, though, exactly what kind of garments such natural materials ought to constitute? The answer—trousers and shirts—may at first seem anti-climactic. But when one considers that a manufacturer who bothers to use natural materials will likely bother about other details as well, one sees there is hope for more interesting tailoring, more elaborate ornamentation, and overall greater diversity in such garb.[16] Finally, in addition to the practical advantages of natural materials that also happen to yield great aesthetic gains, there is a quasi-sacramental fittingness in man's use of them. Man, chosen to till the garden of creation, appears well in materials so evidently the fruits of that garden. Synthetics, on the other hand, will always have a subtly emasculating effect; they are wrappings for soft men who, cowed by the machine's efficiency, have relinquished their rightful stewardship and have lost the will to bear up manfully under the curse of Adam.

Dressing well each day, albeit in the modern suit or some other respectable style, as the occasion requires, mounts a rejection of philistinism, of rationalism, of the apathetic stupor in which most men live. This practice begins the return to truly beautiful dress. These humble garments—the suit, the collared shirt, the wool coat, the fedora—are simply placeholders, things chosen as better options in a world filled with abysmal ones. If the modern suit leaves men discontent, perhaps longing for the vivid hues of the Krakowian peasants, or the exquisite refinement of the *ancien régime*, this is the first sign of hope; it means that men have begun to see through the fog. They realize that what they've been told was useless has a meaning so profound that its use extends to the very health of the soul. They come to see that what they've been told was a waste of time is actually a glimmer of eternity. It is a vision paid for with the painful discontent that accompanies it. But that pain is a small price to pay for the parting of the fog that allows a man to see the world as it really is. In this light of reality, he may begin his noble work of restoration.

---

[16] There is also much benefit in men's reclaiming the traditional dress of their heritage. Even now, one sees men of Scottish descent wearing kilts on formal occasions to fine effect.

9

Recommended Reading and Critiques

N THE YEARS I HAVE WRITTEN ON DRESS, I have read various books on the topic by Catholics and non-Catholics alike. This chapter contains my reviews of some of these books. In the world of literary critique, it sometimes happens that the best books receive the shortest reviews, and this is the case here. The books that I found disappointing receive longer reviews because criticism demands explanation. My hope is that, in reading of my disagreements with certain authors, my readers may further digest the topics at hand. Now, on to one of the very best books:

The Lost Art of Dress by Linda Przybyszewski (BASIC BOOKS, 2014)

If you were to read only one book on dress, this is the one to read. Read it once; read it twice; keep it on your nightstand. It's a tour de force of history and pithy artistic instruction delivered with humor and wit. It's a lark that will you leave you laughing but also thinking deeply. You'll find it smashes myths about dress and shines light on universal sartorial truths. One cannot come away without renewed excitement. Despite her gloomy title, Przybyszewski convinces her readers that dress is an art that, if they so choose, need not be lost!

Art in Everyday Life by Harriet and Vetta Goldstein (THE MACMILLAN COMPANY, 1930)

With *Art in Everyday Life*, one can enjoy an immersion into the same waters with which Linda Przybyszewski so delightfully splashes us in *The Lost Art of Dress*. This book provides a thorough, never tedious, tour through the Art Principles with a multitude of illustrations that perfectly concretize each point. In addition to dress, *Art in Everyday Life* covers a swath of topics from interior design to city planning. By analyzing each art principle in a variety of contexts, the Goldsteins highlight the universality of the art principles and demonstrate how artistic thinking can become a habit that shapes our everyday lives. This book is an excellent resource for anyone looking for a more substantial understanding of artistic principles and may even be a perfect choice for a homeschool art curriculum. It was, in fact, a textbook in colleges of home economics for decades.

Principles of Correct Dress by Florence Hull Winterburn, Jean Philippe Worth, Paul Poiret (KESSINGER'S LEGACY REPRINTS, 2010)

Few books describe dress as an art more emphatically than *Principles of Correct Dress*. A 1914 compilation by Florence Hull Winterburn, Jean Philippe Worth, and Paul Poiret, this little work admonishes its readers to seek all that is becoming to the individual rather than adhering to the dictates of fleeting and unflattering fashion. Jean Philippe Worth cites the world's great portraits displayed in "picture galleries" as fonts of inspiration: "Such great painters as Nattier, Madame Lebrun, Romney, Lawrence, and Gainsborough serve again and again as aids to the costumier in color, design, and trimming."[1]

The book goes on to describe in no mincing terms the principles which ought to guide women in regard to their complexion, their stature, their age, and their activities. For its treatment of color alone, the book is a gem, presenting all kinds of fascinating palettes and acquainting its readers with famous portraits (easily searched online) that illustrate successful use of these color schemes.

Paul Poiret closes the work with his ten precepts on dress, which all boil down to one thing: *decorum*—that art of decorating the world with oneself and one's actions. Not one of the book's three authors offers a passing glance at the god of self-esteem; for honest men and women of art, satisfaction comes from the truth. They offer no platitudes about inner beauty or self-worth to stout women or sallow

---

[1]   Winterburn et al., *Principles of Correct Dress* (Kessinger's, 2010), 50.

women or old women. Rather, they provide ample guidance on just what such women should wear.

There is in these pages a most refreshing common sense that bravely looks the fallen world (and all that falls short of ideals) in the face and applies, as deftly as any physician administering his balm, the principles of art and good taste.

Christian Fashion by Virginia Coda Nunziante
(CALX MARIAE PUBLISHING, 2022)

The art of dress will always have a moral as well as an aesthetic component, and the moral component precedes the aesthetic one — i.e., a practitioner of the art of dress, if he desires the salvation of souls, must decide he will work within the bounds of decency. In her short work, *Christian Fashion*, Virginia Coda Nunziante has compiled the most saliant writings of churchmen on the moral considerations of dress. She begins the work with an introduction of her own authorship that sets the stage for a presentation of writings from Benedict XV, Pius XI, Pius XII, Giuseppe Cardinal Siri, and Giovanni Cardinal Colombo. The texts are unabridged, and, aside from a lucid introduction, Coda Nunziante does not include any commentary of her own. Rather, she lets the churchmen speak for themselves. This may be to the taste of some, while others may look for more of a conversational approach that provides practical suggestions. But given the confusion surrounding these same Church statements on dress, *Christian Fashion* is a fine resource for its convenient compilation of essential Vatican documents translated beautifully into English. It is an excellent complement (or prerequisite) for those furthering their exploration of dress as an art and for those conducting research in this area.

"A Theology of Dress" by Erik Peterson (*Communio*, Fall 1993)

In this brilliant essay, Erik Peterson goes beyond the level of basic morality to probe the topic of dress more deeply. While recognizing the moral component of dress, he warns his readers against a simplistic treatment of the topic with the following insight:

> The reality is that this question touches upon the most central truths of the Christian faith and that, therefore,

> any attempt to settle what is basically a metaphysical and theological question by neat moral reasoning is bound to fail. An approach given solely to opposing immoral dress cannot possibly see the problem in its full outline.[2]

The essay goes on to shed light on the metaphysical change that took place in man's nature as a result of the fall and points out man's response: to clothe himself. The fall, Peterson writes, did not make previously naked flesh suddenly visible; rather, it denuded flesh that was previously clothed in God's glory, thus making it naked. Man's desire to clothe himself reflects the reality of his being ordered to the "addition of grace and completion by means of it."[3] Peterson's essay is worth reading many times over in order to contemplate the deep philosophical truths unearthed in it. Before hurrying to promote standards for modest dress, one ought to understand why we dress in the first place and what dress means for man. Peterson's essay deftly answers these questions.

Aesthetics (in two volumes) by Dietrich von Hildebrand
(DIETRICH VON HILDEBRAND LEGACY PROJECT, 2016)

While I have already highly recommended books on art (i.e., *The Lost Art of Dress*, *Art in Everyday Life*, and *Principles of Correct Dress*), I encourage those wishing to learn still more, and especially those taking part in the design and production of clothing, to immerse themselves in the aesthetics of Dietrich von Hildebrand. This Catholic philosopher, the son of a renowned sculptor who enjoyed an idyllic childhood in Florence, knew like few others what beauty as manifested by art can do for the soul. Even as he looked back and recognized the devastating impact of the Industrial Revolution on the very life of man, he experienced firsthand the terrible destruction that the Second World War wreaked on Europe. Hildebrand's response was neither dismissive of the deep loss he saw increasing daily around him, nor a call to arms with practical solutions. He simply defended the importance of beauty for human happiness and, as evidence for his claims, called upon an astonishing wealth

---

[2] Erik Peterson, "A Theology of Dress," *Communio* 20.3 (Fall 1993): 559.
[3] Peterson quoting Hedwig Conrad Martius, 562.

of artistic examples known to him from his travels throughout Europe. Although his pages dedicated to dress are relatively few, every paragraph of his two volumes promotes a sensitivity to beauty and respect for true art that will prove an invaluable foundation for those designing or selecting clothing.

The Classical Vernacular by Roger Scruton (CARCANET PRESS, 1994)

This collection of essays is focused entirely on architecture, but the sound aesthetic reasoning (not to mention clever writing) so characteristic of Scruton combine to make the work a delight to read for any aspiring artist. In fact, curious similarities exist between architectural design and sartorial design. Both buildings and clothing must satisfy the demands of function and form. And, insofar as good architecture provides a beautiful abode for man that, at the same time, looks well on the street, it is just a larger, grander, more permanent kind of clothing. Buildings, like people, ought to have good manners, Scruton points out. It is rude and uncivilized for a building to look shabby or shocking or otherwise out-of-place to passersby. The same is true for dress. Thus, principles of architecture make a fascinating study for anyone practicing the art of dress.

The Vision of the Soul by James Matthew Wilson
(CATHOLIC UNIVERSITY OF AMERICA PRESS, 2017)

The scope of practical applications one may draw from *The Vision of the Soul* is as broad as the book's insights are profound. James Matthew Wilson's analysis of beauty, which leverages Eco and Maritain among other giants, fills in the metaphysical blanks left by more practical books such as *The Lost Art of Dress* and *Art in Everyday Life*. For instance, where, in the latter book, the authors are content to describe the sense of "repose" or "satisfaction"[4] experienced in the apprehension of a successful design, Wilson writes the following with philosophical precision:

> The state of simultaneous passivity and activity that perceives immediately the form of truth is one where the mind

---

[4] Goldstein, *Art in Everyday Life*, 83, 119, 226.

rests in perception of a formal whole in itself and in all its
harmonious relations with the whole of reality, and this,
we have said, is beauty.[5]

While *The Vision of the Soul* will challenge most readers with its flights
of metaphysics, the challenge is well worth the effort. The book's
treatment of form alone is too good to miss for anyone serious about
understanding the aesthetics of dress.

Fig Leaves Are Not Enough by Dom Pius Mary Noonan, OSB (CANA PRESS, 2024)

This book is formatted as a series of letters exchanged between
the author and a young lady directee regarding topics of modesty
and dress. Noonan's advice is fatherly—at once kind and firm, and
always discreet. He draws on Scriptural sources, scientific studies,
and the aforementioned Vatican documents on dress. Noonan does
not shy away from quoting the highly controversial note issued in
1930 by the Sacred Congregation of the Council:

> A dress cannot be called decent which is cut deeper than
> two fingers' breadth under the pit of the throat, which
> does not cover the arms at least to the elbows, and scarcely
> reaches a bit below the knee. Furthermore, dresses made
> of transparent material are improper.[6]

These none too vague guidelines are often referred to as "The Vatican Standards," the "Objective Norms of Decent Dress," or "The
Standards of Marylike Dress," and they have caused much conten-
tion among Catholics over the years. Many critics complain that
these standards are prudish and rooted in a bygone day.

However, anyone who has sought to teach the practice of modest dress will have discovered that objective norms can be very
helpful, and it is thus understandable why Noonan and other
directors of souls may wish to emphasize the Vatican Standards.
Society has become so desensitized to immodesty that without
clear, almost mathematical guidelines, some women just setting

---

[5] James Matthew Wilson, *The Vision of the Soul* (Catholic University of America
Press, 2017), 101.
[6] Pius Mary Noonan, O.S.B., *Fig Leaves Are Not Enough* (Cana Press, 2024), 71.

out on the road will not be able to guess just how conservative their clothing should actually be.

There are some nuances, however, that Noonan does not take into account. For instance, practical experience and history show that a neckline lower than the "two fingers' breadth" can still be decent. Take, for example, Servant of God Empress Zita who wore gowns cut away more than two fingers at the neckline. No one can honestly call any of her gowns immodest, and it would have been a great loss of graceful elegance had the exquisite necklines been cut differently. It is true a neckline should not be much lower than two fingers—three, maybe four fingers. It depends on the woman and it depends on the dress, but Noonan does not state this. He treats the standards as quite precisely fixed.

A subtler but actually larger shortcoming in an otherwise helpful book is Noonan's oversimplification of visible beauty:

> You asked me about dresses that flow down to the ankles and the wrists. I will be honest and say that it would make me happy to know that you are dressed that way. There is no more beautiful sight on earth, admirable to behold.[7]

These are the words of a good and earnest priest, but they'll fail to satisfy many a reader because they don't account for the fact that dresses have aesthetic qualities as well as moral ones. A long dress *may* be beautiful to behold—or it may not be. Unfortunately, in this day and age, such dresses are not well-designed and are often sadly unappealing to wearer and viewers alike. What Noonan ought to have told his readers is that the modest choice made with a heart seeking God will always possess a moral beauty. However, moral beauty is not the same as artistic success. There are moral goods (the goods to be done), and there are artistic goods (the goods to be made), and both are worth striving for. One does not guarantee the other. True beauty in its fullest sense is a combination of moral and artistic beauty, but, to achieve this, one must learn dress as an art, and one must develop good taste.

---

[7] Noonan, 70.

These things—art and taste—are hard to learn and harder to teach. It's much easier to tell someone that beauty equates to following the Vatican Standards, but such a method ultimately does not serve the cause.

Catholic Modesty by Jacinta Boudreau
(SELF-PUBLISHED; SECOND EDITION)

In *Catholic Modesty*, Jacinta Boudreau explores Church teachings on modesty and how these apply to many present-day questions such as dress, comportment, our choices of entertainment, and our treatment of marriage, procreation, and the marriage bed. The book's chapters on history present timelines of events in the world and the Church that shaped the clothing and entertainment industries and ultimately eroded decency. Boudreau's sources overlap considerably with those used by Noonan in *Fig Leaves Are Not Enough*, but Boudreau casts a wider net and includes many more supporting documents from patristic times to the present day. It should also be noted that the female authorship of this book might make the message, though similar to Noonan's, more palatable to certain readers. Like *Fig Leaves Are Not Enough*, *Catholic Modesty* considers dress almost entirely in terms of morality, which, though it leaves dress as an art untouched, is perhaps a necessary prerequisite in a society where decency does not come as a matter of course and the most time-honored conventions have long been jettisoned.

Dressing with Dignity by Colleen Hammond (TAN BOOKS, 2005)

First published in 2004 with a second edition in 2005, *Dressing with Dignity* precedes *Fig Leaves Are Not Enough* and *Catholic Modesty* and is perhaps the most well-known "modesty" book on the market. As its title implies, Colleen Hammond's book is focused on femininity and dignity. It covers the same general topics as do the other two books, and its sources are the usual variety of Vatican documents, Church teachings, and historical and scientific surveys.

Hammond deserves credit for rising to an enormous challenge, namely, the treatment of dress in the early 2000s when the fashions were sliding further and further to obscenity and few Catholics (least of all clergy and bishops) had anything helpful to say about it. Even if only for her presentation of certain studies (tracking the eye movements of men) that confirm the seductive effects of women's pants and slitted skirts, *Dressing with Dignity* may be called a useful manual.[8] No doubt, for those who are really looking for answers and some firm guidelines, Hammond's book fills the gap.

However, besides those souls looking for someone to decry the world's sartorial indecencies, there are many more who are not entirely convinced that they wish to dress modestly—or, at least, who are not convinced that they wish to dress like the well-meaning, somewhat frumpy woman who gave them the book in the first place. These are the readers who, not necessarily from promiscuity or vice, but from a deep longing for something beautiful, will find Colleen Hammond's book unconvincing.

The main problem is that Hammond's treatment of modesty falls prey to some oversimplifications that darken, rather than illuminate, the question of how to dress. "A shirt is not attractive or demure if it dips lower than two fingers' width below your collarbone," Hammond states.[9] This claim is simply not true. Throughout the course of costume history, there have been deeper necklines that are attractive, demure, and spectacularly beautiful. Some have been decent and some indecent depending on their extremity, but one cannot expect a reasoning reader to swallow the claim that nothing outside of the two fingers' standard is beautiful and simply move on from there. Artists and those with knowledge of costume history will have particular difficulty with this claim. Like it or not, the crew neck is one of the most unflattering necklines ever devised.[10] And yet, writers like Hammond would have readers believe the style is virtually a guaranteed sartorial success simply because of the coverage it offers. *Sometimes*, revealing clothing makes the wearer appear unattractive, vulgar, and far from beautiful. On the other hand, *sometimes* (especially for younger women) revealing clothing sets off the wearer in a very attractive way. The real challenge, then, is to

[8] Collen Hammond, *Dressing with Dignity*, second ed. (TAN Books, 2005), 49–50.
[9] Hammond, 96.
[10] Przybyszewski, *Lost Art of Dress* (Basic Books, 2014), 233–34.

educate readers on how to dress in a way that is not immodest and yet still flattering to the human figure and pleasing to the human eye. This harmonious accord struck between prudence and art requires careful formation in the principles of art and years of development of good taste.[11] Sweeping statements and crude measurement rules like those presented by Hammond will not suffice.

In addition to its faulty analysis, another flaw that weakens the effectiveness of *Dressing with Dignity* is its cloying, colloquial style. For instance, Hammond concludes a brief mention of St. Paul's passage on "how she may please her husband" (1 Cor 7:34) with the blithe quip, "So, married ladies, feel free to look attractive for your hubby!"[12]—a statement that leaves unmarried women in doubt as to whether they are allowed to look attractive given they have not yet found a "hubby." Later, Hammond causes further consternation with an infelicitous statement that seems to make dress nothing but a kind of fishing for men's attention: "One last note: Get an apron to wear in the kitchen. Don't laugh! It's amazing how different you will feel in an apron. And, for some reason, most men love it!"[13]

Unfortunately, stylistic blunders such as these are irritating enough to cause many a woman to close the book and vow never to worry about modesty again. *Dressing with Dignity* will likely only satisfy those virtuous souls already totally disposed to virtuous dress and able to patiently sift through the book's foibles.

Worthy of Wearing by Nicole Caruso (SOPHIA INSTITUTE PRESS, 2021)

In the winter of 2022, as part of an attempt to acquaint myself with contemporary Catholic literature on dress, I obtained Nicole Caruso's *Worthy of Wearing*. At first, its buttery hardcover, wealth of full-page photos, and clean, modern design impressed me. However, I soon became frustrated searching its pages in vain for the answer to the question of what marks the difference between worthy clothing and unworthy clothing. This question has deep philosophical

---

[11] It is this accumulated wisdom that can only come with time that makes a mother's and even a grandmother's roles so vital in teaching young girls how to dress.
[12] Hammond, *Dressing with Dignity*, 27.   [13] Hammond, 85.

implications that deserve thorough consideration. It is the question to which Catholic writers on dress should devote their talents today, and Caruso's title arouses high hopes that her book does so. Unfortunately, this is not the case.

Instead, *Worthy of Wearing* perfectly exemplifies that unfortunate new genre of book we might call Catholic Women's Self-Help. Peppered with plenty of autobiographical references, quotes from St. John Paul II, The Little Flower, and St. Josemaría Escrivá, alongside the occasional "mindset check," the book's theology reaches about the kindergarten level: you were made by God; therefore, you have dignity. In no more illuminating terms, the cloying message slops the reader again and again. "Do you know you're beautiful? I know you are," Caruso says.[14] And elsewhere adds, "I want you to be empowered by just how worthy you are."[15]

As regards the kind of dress the book promotes, one is at first overwhelmed by the burgeoning array of possibilities. From dresses, skirts, and blouses, to leather leggings, combat boots, body suits, and miniskirts (worn, of course, with your Chanel broach and Marian consecration chain), one begins to imagine that just about anything goes. Skinny jeans, ripped jeans, sleeveless, cleavage, skin tight, above the knee, below the knee, sweet and demure, or splayed out in menswear—it's all good. Everything is good, the book seems to say, leaving us wondering why we need a book to tell us this when the world already does. The only mistake, we're warned, is to think we ourselves are not good. Even when it comes to modesty, if your intentions are good, you're golden—a far cry (too far) from the infamous Vatican Standards.[16]

While the handwaving approach in *Worthy of Wearing* is disappointing, its general vapidity when it comes to aesthetics and theology is far more concerning. The good news is that most readers will come away so hungry that they'll surely continue their search for the truth. It is now the duty of Catholic writers and artists to devote greater time and attention to the topic of dress and, thus, provide their readers with better guidance.

[14] Nicole M. Caruso, *Worthy of Wearing* (Sophia Institute Press, 2021), 77.
[15] Caruso, 56.   [16] See Hammond, *Dressing with Dignity.*

The Catholic Wardrobe by Meghan Ashley Sokolowski
(SELF-PUBLISHED, 2020)

Meghan Sokolowski's manual on dress has a promising start with a quotation from a religious superior: "For human persons, clothing is symbolic: it is a sign of who I am and who I wish to be. What we wear forms us." With such a profound start, one might expect the book to flow into profound analysis and lead to many practical applications. Unfortunately, this is not the case. "I'm no philosopher or theologian (obviously)," Sokolowski admits. "I'm a fashion stylist."[17]

The book might have, with a fashion stylist's experience, still contained quite useful artistic lessons. Again, the reader's expectations are dashed. Sokolowski nowhere identifies the real crux of the problem of dress today: namely, that the market does not produce beautiful clothing, and that women have lost the practice of making their own. Rather, Sokolowski perpetuates the mistaken belief that materialism is to be blamed, that the market gives us too many options: "In our modern world, we are saturated with options, without education or any thoughtful inspiration on which pieces to build your wardrobe around. We are inundated like never before!!!"[18]

On the surface, Sokolowski's statement is true. There is overproduction of clothing, as any environmentalist would tell you. However, it's overproduction of trash. Yes, most clothing produced today is trash before it ever reaches a store's or an Amazon warehouse's shelves. Needless to say, very little of the clothing sold on the market today is a valid option for a Catholic woman. This is the vital nuance that Sokolowski just misses. She theorizes that women become overwhelmed merely by the sheer volume of clothing pieces available to them rather than presenting the true state of affairs: women are discontented because nothing they buy, no matter how much they buy, is actually beautiful. In her manual of sweet photos, excessive exclamation points, generic tips on body types, and guides on closet editing, she, like Caruso, cheers her readers on to finding their "personal style" without helping them learn anything about objective principles of art or beauty. The clothing she promotes in

---

[17] Meghan Ashley Sokolowski, *The Catholic Wardrobe* (2020), 6.
[18] Sokolowski, 10.

her example photos clearly shows that, far from condemning the sad state of contemporary design, she subscribes to an "anything goes" approach.

In summary, *The Catholic Wardrobe* is another vapid if not misleading book on dress that misses the main problems and, as a result, falls far short of tangible solutions.

The Theology of Style by Lillian Fallon (ASCENSION, 2023)

Lillian Fallon's *Theology of Style* is a sort of memoir detailing the evolution of her views on the body, fashion, and modesty. As may be guessed by the book's title, Fallon pays homage to St. John Paul II's collection of teachings called *Theology of the Body*. She relates how, in a university course, Michael Waldstein introduced her to the teachings, which subsequently validated her profound love of dress. Fallon's book, at a slim 129 pages, focuses on one salient truth from the pope's many lengthy addresses: the body manifests the soul. Fallon explains her own awakening in the light of this truth as follows:

> For years, I subconsciously thought that my body restricted my soul and that every time I put together an outfit, I limited myself to drawing attention to the materialism of my body and my clothes. But St. John Paul II reveals that the materiality of the body is necessary for the expression of the soul.... Again, I couldn't help but see the correlation to personal style. Because the body manifests the soul and the soul is expressed through our bodies, the things we choose to wear can communicate the invisible beauty of the soul while dignifying the visible beauty of the body.[19]

This indeed is a wonderful truth, and many Catholic women can point to similar distinct moments when they grasped the real reason to love the act of clothing themselves. The understanding of body-soul unity is what gives us as Catholics the permission and *mission* to cultivate dress as an art. It gives us the right and the duty to

---

[19] Lillian Fallon, *Theology of Style* (Ascension Books, 2023), 10.

be concerned with the good to be made, i.e., the work of art that is an ensemble of clothing.[20]

In her section on art, Fallon is at pains to explain why dress, or, as she terms it, style, *is* an art. All well and good, but, unfortunately, she seizes on a personalist approach to art that, as I will later show, does not lead to a restoration of beautiful dress. Fallon lauds the following passage from John Paul's *Letter to Artists*:

> In producing a work, artists express themselves to the point where their work becomes a unique disclosure of their own being, of what they are and of how they are.... In shaping a masterpiece, the artist not only summons his work into being, but also in some way reveals his own personality by means of it.[21]

This concept becomes Fallon's springboard by which she reaches the same hackneyed conclusion beaten dead already by Caruso and Sokolowski: namely, dress is ultimately about personal expression.[22] Hence the subtitle of this book: *Expressing the Unique and Unrepeatable You.*

It's a disappointing conclusion in any book, but most of all in one that promises theology and seems to pay some tribute to art. Whether or not art "reveals the artist" is beside the point and should be of little concern to the artist. When Blessed Fra Angelico wept with sorrow and joy each time he painted a fresco of the Crucifixion, one suspects that his mind was not on expressing his personality; rather, he had forgotten himself altogether. Incidentally, Fallon does not cite Fra Angelico; she cites van Gogh and his self-portraits.[23]

Even so, one may argue that dress, not being a representational art, in contrast to, say, sculpture or fresco, will necessarily result in personal expression. Indeed, the very materials of the art of dress consist of a human and his clothes. This is true enough, but there will still be governing principles that should steer the artist to the

---

[20] See *Summa theologiae*, I-II, Q. 57, art. 3.
[21] Fallon, *Theology of Style*, 30–31, quoting John Paul II's *Letter to Artists*.
[22] See Caruso's *Worthy of Wearing* and Sokolowski's *The Catholic Wardrobe*.
[23] Fallon, *Theology of Style*, 31.

good, rather than his own idiosyncratic whims. Fallon does not state this, but, rather, seems to promote the opposite view. She cautions against formulas or methods for seeking an ideal, saying that by promoting this "rigid standard," one treats women as "objects, like malleable mounds of clay that need to be molded into perfect proportions to have value."[24]

It's clear that Fallon's intent is to uphold the dignity of being. She is reacting against the secular fashion industry that pays no heed to the human soul and thus perverts the quest for the beautification of the body. Unfortunately, she mixes up the ontological with the aesthetical and concludes that to honestly and dispassionately recognize a lack of ideal beauty in a material thing (a body) is to dismiss its value altogether. Rather than considering whether there might be profound spiritual meaning behind the "need for perfect proportion" and rising to the challenge of translating this yearning to a way of dress that promotes the good to be made without losing sight of the good to be done, Fallon simply dismisses any such yearnings as unnecessary and outright harmful.

Here she falls into the trap of almost every other Catholic dress commentator today: because the fashion industry poses certain rules (themselves perverted and idiosyncratic), she proposes to cast aside all rules; because the fashion industry promotes an ideal, she dismisses all ideals. This misthought reaction against "the industry" becomes a sort of aesthetical anarchy that throws the baby out with the bathwater. It's an approach that will never produce a culture of beauty because it pays no respect to form. Ironically, the products of such a philosophy will differ little in appearance from the fashions of the very industry it attempts to reject. After all, that industry too pays no respect to form.

Theology of Style extracts the bread-and-butter truths from *Theology of the Body* with which many Catholic readers will be familiar: self-gift as the way to human happiness, self-sacrifice as necessary in all human love, complementarity of men and women, etc. In theory, Fallon's theology does not deviate from John Paul II's teachings.

[24] Fallon, 113.

However, her applications lead one to wonder whether she really understands the nature of this pope's work.

"I don't care," Fallon replied when a woman informed her that her hot pink eye shadow wasn't flattering. "She was surprised at my response," Fallon goes on to explain, "thinking I was offended and defensive but really, I just wanted to share that I truly didn't care if it wasn't flattering. Yes, a different eyeshadow would have brought out my eyes better, but I didn't want to wear it. I wanted to wear pink eyeshadow."[25]

Throughout her book, Fallon uses similar vignettes to celebrate her exercise of self-expression; this self-expression she believes is the manifestation of her soul (and therefore irrefutably good). She never pauses to consider whether we, as human artists and not divine artists, may sometimes make an artistic blunder or betray a need for improvement in good taste. Nor, outside of her discussion of modesty, does she consider the charity owed to her neighbor. That is, we who dress ought first to consider the sensibilities of those who have to look at us. This common-sense fraternal charity goes in tandem with John Paul's teachings on self-gift and making good use of our freedom in Christ.[26] Until the Sexual Revolution, virtually all commentators on dress emphasized the duty, to put it bluntly, not to make oneself a public eyesore.[27]

Fallon contrasts Audrey Hepburn as a positive role model of "style" against Lady Gaga whom Fallon identifies as a mere tool of fashion. Hepburn's style expressed interior beauty and a loveable personality, Fallon asserts, whereas Lady Gaga, with her outlandish choices, only expresses ideologies.[28] However, when Fallon vaunts her own garish makeup, she seems not to realize that, of the two celebrities, Lady Gaga, and not Audrey Hepburn, would wear hot pink eye shadow. The author of *Theology of Style* seems unaware that her program of self-expression plays into the hands of the very same ideologues who put Lady Gaga in a dress of meat.

---

[25] Fallon, 112.

[26] John Paul II, *Man and Woman He Created Them: A Theology of the Body*, 53:1–3, trans. Michael Waldstein (Pauline Books & Media, 2006), 339–40.

[27] Przybyszewski, *Lost Art of Dress*, 78.   [28] Fallon, *Theology of Style*, 16.

Fallon's treatment of modesty is, not surprisingly, against measurement systems such as the two fingers' breadth test. She emphasizes the importance of modesty, but views it as something not appropriate to boil down to rules and regulations. Citing the practices of baring the midriff in India and baring the breasts in Africa, Fallon covers the well-trodden ground of "cultural norms." She cites the 1992 catechism approvingly and Pius XI dubiously. She acknowledges the importance of covering the sexual organs but questions the need to cover knees, shoulders, "a cleavage-free chest." "At what point is it a 'him' problem?" Fallon asks when pointing out the need for male custody of the eyes and mind. "What is the difference between 'normal' temptation and perversion?"[29]

Admittedly, Fallon deserves credit for casting light on a problem many scrupulous persons encounter: namely, a hyper-focus on sexuality that tends to make the act of dressing feel like navigating an obstacle course riddled with landmines of mortal sin. She also does well to ask some hard questions about male responsibility, which is something found in few other books on modesty. Fallon strikes on the truth that, when living in a hyper-sexualized society where vice and perversion abound, the best antidote for any woman is to fight the urge to think in a hyper-sexualized way herself.

Nevertheless, the treatment of modesty in *Theology of Style* is ultimately disappointing. Fallon drifts off course with phrases like "a healthy application of modesty,"[30] as if this virtue were a drug or carcinogen. In another passage she says, "I choose to use the word 'reverence' over 'modesty.' This word implies a positive truth about the female body, rather than negativity."[31] Eager to clear the way for self-expressive dress, Fallon does nothing to provide her readers with real answers to the hard questions. For instance, why, if crop tops are sometimes permissible (a claim Fallon makes),[32] do they have no precedent in any Christian culture? Or, what do pants on women (which Fallon approves) express about a woman's soul? Giuseppe Cardinal Siri wrote on the problems stemming from women's use of men's styles back in 1960,[33] but if Fallon had cared to reference

---

29 Fallon, 99.   30 Fallon, 102.   31 Fallon, 106.   32 Fallon, 110.
33 Siri, *Christian Fashion*, 98–106.

Cardinal Siri, she doubtless would have treated him as skeptically as she treats Pius XI.[34]

In summary, *Theology of Style* neither does justice to John Paul II's *Theology of the Body* nor promotes a sound artistic approach to dress. Readers looking to learn from the sainted pope's addresses might go directly to the source, particularly passages on purity and modesty.[35] When it comes to cultivating the virtue of art, that true understanding of the good to be made, readers would do well to worry a little less about self-expression and a little more about self-sacrifice.

ADDITIONAL RESOURCES

Daniel Roche, *The Culture of Clothing: Dress and Fashion in the Ancien Régime* (Cambridge University Press, 1994)

Umberto Eco, *The Aesthetics of Thomas Aquinas* (Harvard University Press, 1988)

Jacques Maritain, *Art and Scholasticism* [1920] (Cluny Media, 2020)

Abigail Kengor, "Modesty vs. Androgyny," *Crisis Magazine*, January 23, 2023, https://www.crisismagazine.com/opinion/modesty-vs-androgyny

Thomas Storck, "Seeking Beauty in Art: Some Implications of a Thomistic Statement about Glass Saws," in idem, *From Christendom to Americanism and Beyond* (Angelico Press, 2015)

Marcus Berquist, "On the Signification of Clothes," in idem, *Learning and Discipleship: The Collected Papers of Marcus R. Berquist* (Thomas Aquinas College, 2019), 486–88

Sebastian Morello, "On Not Looking Awful," in idem, *Unto the Ages of Ages: Essays on Political Traditionalism* (Arouca Press, 2025), 157–62; also online at *The European Conservative*, February 17, 2024, https://europeanconservative.com/articles/essay/on-not-looking-awful-the-three-sartorial-basics/

Catherine Rose, "Why Modesty?," *Catholic Answers*, March 1, 2024, https://www.catholic.com/magazine/online-edition/why-modesty

---

34 Fallon, *Theology of Style, 95–96.*
35 John Paul II, *Man and Woman He Created Them,* 50:1–3 and 57:1–3.

Katie Łastowiecka, "The Met Gala and Modern Beauty," *Crisis Magazine*, May 16, 2024, https://crisismagazine.com/opinion/the-met-gala-and-modern-beauty

Maria Madise, "Can Christian decency be guarded in the summertime?," *Voice of the Family*, May 29, 2024, https://voiceofthefamily.com/can-christian-decency-be-guarded-in-the-summertime/

Regina Doman, "The Elements of a Woman's Dress," Parts 1 and 2, *The Culture Recovery Journals*, July 25 and July 31, 2024, https://reginadoman.substack.com/p/the-elements-of-a-womans-dress-part; https://reginadoman.substack.com/p/elements-of-a-womans-dress-part-2

Anna Davis, "Changing the World, One Outfit at a Time," *Crisis Magazine*, August 23, 2024, https://crisismagazine.com/opinion/changing-the-world-one-outfit-at-a-time

Virginia Coda Nunziante, "Pope Pius XII on Fashion," *Voice of the Family*, August 21, 2024, https://voiceofthefamily.com/pope-pius-xii-on-fashion/

Erik Dahlberg, "Helping One's 'Self': The Great Controversy of Cutlery," *The European Conservative*, December 8, 2024, https://europeanconservative.com/articles/essay/helping-ones-self-the-great-controversy-of-cutlery/

Peter Kwasniewski, "Deliberately Dressing Up," *Tradition and Sanity* Substack, June 10, 2024, https://www.traditionsanity.com/p/deliberately-dressing-up

APPENDIX
Where to Shop?

AFTER WRITING A BOOK THAT CALLS for a return to very high standards of dress, one naturally feels an aversion to come down from the mountain and actually recommend some places to shop here and now. Any clothing brand in this day is sure to disappoint in one way or another.

For this reason, I say again that we should seek to design and sew our own clothing. But here again is a dream indulged in the clouds. At least for now, even the most zealous dreamers have to come down from the clouds and dress for work on Monday.

Below is my list of brands I have gathered over the years that have served to aid me in this humble effort of dressing for work on Monday, even as I've dreamed of something better. In addition to these, and perhaps serving to satisfy me more than any retailer below, are antique stores and vintage clothing vendors. Certainly, it's difficult to find just the right thing from such shops, but when one does, it's a red-letter day.

Note: Not all items sold by these retailers are modest, tasteful, and feminine. Be selective.

XIAOLIZI (shopxiaolizi.com)

I recommend Xiaolizi for its classical designs and high-quality fabrics (linen or cotton/linen blends for summer and wool blends for winter). I recommend custom sizing, but the made-to-order pieces can work.

SIMPLE RETRO (simpleretro.com)

Look for the 100% cotton dresses for summer and 100% wool items for winter. Some of the polyester pieces are adequate, but it's a shame they don't have higher quality fabrics. Still a fun little store.

ETNOSOUL (etnosoul.com.ua)

I love the natural fibers and embroidery of these pieces.

Here are a few more places to check:
House of Bruar (houseofbruar.com)
Smock London (smocklondon.com)
Betty Hannah (bettyhannah.com)
Sezane (sezane.com)
eShakti (eshakti.com)
Pettalush (petallush.com)
Ivy City Co (ivycityco.com)
CHICWISH (chicwish.com)
Brooks Brothers (brooksbrothers.com)
Draper James (draperjames.com)
SLIPINTOSOFT (slipintosoft.com)
Jolly Vintage (jolly-vintage.com)
Son de Flor (sondeflor.com)
Vermont Country Store (vermontcountrystore.com)
Dainty Jewells (daintyjewells.com)
JanieLanie (janielanie.com)
Florence Adams (florenceadams.com)
Marylike Dresses (facebook.com/profile.php?id=61564862050808)

Shoe resources:
American Duchess (americanduchess.com)
Re-mix Vintage (remixvintageshoes.com)

Swimwear:
Calypsa (calypsa.com)
Urban Modesty (urbanmodesty.com)

ABOUT THE AUTHOR

MISS ANNA KALINOWSKA left an eight-year career in the aerospace industry to devote herself full-time to the restoration of Christian culture. She has contributed regularly to *One Peter Five* and *New Liturgical Movement*, and this is her first book. When not writing on aesthetics, she works as a liturgical artist at an oratory in her native St. Louis where she designs vestments, altar dressings, and floral arrangements for the glory of God. She also leads workshops in traditional social dance nationwide and often hosts folk dances and formal balls to celebrate Church feasts.

www.ingramcontent.com/pod-product-compliance
Lightning Source LLC
Chambersburg PA
CBHW050004040726
47599CB00014B/1204